Educating the Gifted

Get inspired, learn from others, and reflect on the joy of making a difference with *Educating the Gifted: Wisdom and Insights for Inspired Teaching*.

Covering topics such as identification, equity in access and opportunity, teacher growth, advocacy, and more, this book shares moments of joy, practical strategies, and effective tips for advanced learning from expert practitioners and leaders who work with gifted students. Each chapter begins with a brief exploration of an issue or concept, followed by a series of related strategies and ideas, and ends with delightful, joyful stories from a variety of dedicated professionals in the field on what keeps them going through hard days.

This uplifting collection is a must-read for new teachers excited about their upcoming journey, as well as experienced educators and administrators looking to reinvigorate their practice.

Tracy Ford Inman is a consultant in gifted education. She has presented on state, national, and international levels; trained thousands of teachers; published chapters and books, including five TAGT Legacy Award winners; and worked with countless parents. Tracy is a current board member of the two leading national gifted associations, as well as her state organization.

Educating the Gifted
Wisdom and Insights for Inspired Teaching

Tracy Ford Inman

NEW YORK AND LONDON

Designed cover image: © Getty Images

First published 2023
by Routledge
605 Third Avenue, New York, NY 10158

and by Routledge
4 Park Square, Milton Park, Abingdon, Oxon, OX14 4RN

Routledge is an imprint of the Taylor & Francis Group, an informa business

© 2023 Tracy Ford Inman

The right of Tracy Ford Inman to be identified as author of this work has been asserted in accordance with sections 77 and 78 of the Copyright, Designs and Patents Act 1988.

All rights reserved. No part of this book may be reprinted or reproduced or utilised in any form or by any electronic, mechanical, or other means, now known or hereafter invented, including photocopying and recording, or in any information storage or retrieval system, without permission in writing from the publishers.

Trademark notice: Product or corporate names may be trademarks or registered trademarks, and are used only for identification and explanation without intent to infringe.

Library of Congress Cataloging-in-Publication Data
Names: Inman, Tracy F. (Tracy Ford), 1963– author.
Title: Educating the gifted : wisdom and insights for inspired teaching / Tracy Ford Inman.
Description: New York, NY : Routledge, 2023. | Includes bibliographical references. | Summary: Provided by publisher.
Identifiers: LCCN 2022039431 (print) | LCCN 2022039432 (ebook) | ISBN 9781032190761 (hardback) | ISBN 9781032194417 (paperback) | ISBN 9781003259190 (ebook)
Subjects: LCSH: Gifted children—Education. | Teachers of gifted children.
Classification: LCC LC3993 .I59 2023 (print) | LCC LC3993 (ebook) | DDC 371.95—dc23/20221012
LC record available at https://lccn.loc.gov/2022039431
LC ebook record available at https://lccn.loc.gov/2022039432

ISBN: 978-1-032-19076-1 (hbk)
ISBN: 978-1-032-19441-7 (pbk)
ISBN: 978-1-003-25919-0 (ebk)

DOI: 10.4324/9781003259190

Typeset in Palatino
by Apex CoVantage, LLC

This book has been inspired by the always practical yet highly creative Lynette Baldwin. She taught me so much about advocacy, hard work, the necessity of humor, living life with joy, flowers, good china, and friendship. Lynette dedicated her life's work to students with gifts and talents, their educators and administrators, and their families. A tireless advocate for more than 50 years, Lynette taught in a gifted education classroom for 30 years followed by serving as executive director of the Kentucky Association for Gifted Education for 23 years. The worldwide impact she has made is immeasurable. Most people will never know how she changed their lives for the better. But I know, and I am forever grateful.

Contents

Preface viii

1   This Work 1

2   The Talent Scout 4

3   Nurturing and Developing Talent................................ 15

4   Breaking Down Equity Barriers 34

5   The Whole Gifted Child 49

6   The Importance of Educator Growth 72

7   The Advocate 83

8   Looking Through the Lens of Potential 94

    Biographies of Contributors 96

Preface

During these unprecedented times of pandemic, political division, continued inequity, interrupted learning, and exasperated educators, we need some positivity. We need to be reminded of the many joys of our profession; that joy takes various shapes, ranging from utilizing a researched-based strategy that effectively challenges advanced learners or develops healthy partnerships between school and family, to the face of a child who finally owns their unhealthy perfectionism, or the hearty laughter of kids finding others like themselves.

I want *Educating the Gifted: Wisdom and Insights for Inspired Teaching* to tell a narrative of learned wisdom and embraced joy. I want it to be both practical in its advice and shared successes as well as uplifting and encouraging. My hope is that these narratives will be a conduit of revitalization and joy as contributors tell their own stories of practical strategies and effective tips for advanced learning, as well as narrate examples of when they found joy working with these learners, or reflect on how they cultivated joy. The concept of joy tethers the work.

Organized by themes, each chapter addresses an important concept or issue in gifted education: identification, services, equity in access and opportunity, the whole child, teacher growth, and advocacy. Each chapter begins with a brief exploration of the issue or concept, followed by a series of strategies and ideas that directly relate to the topic. Each chapter ends with delightful stories of joy. You will find ideas from a variety of stakeholders, people like you: classroom teachers; educators of gifted students; mental health specialists such as counselors and psychologists; administrators and gifted coordinators; state department gifted personnel; university professors; and leaders in the field, among others. Of course, the experts featured (representing 23 states) are only a small sample of the many dedicated professionals in our field. Each contributor was asked to submit two to five entries and a story of joy.

Please note that Chapter 5: The Whole Gifted Child is longer than the others, containing more strategies, ideas, and stories of joy. Unsurprisingly, the majority of the joy submissions focused on the students themselves – as it should be.

May you be inspired, learn from others, and reflect on your own joys!

1

This Work

It's not too late, you know – it's never too late to learn. We should be lifelong learners, remember? Whether you are a seasoned pro or you just discovered you have your first gifted student in class, I promise you will learn something from this book – some nugget of wisdom, some insight that excites you, that resonates with you, that inspires you. I also believe you will find joy as you read about others' joys. I believe joy, like a yawn, is contagious.

    I always tell my students to make a book their own (as long as it *is* their own, of course) – to highlight passages, underline powerful words and images, jot down questions and reflections, or even dog ear pages (that last one may not work too well with e-books). The more you own the book, making it a part of yourself and your thinking, the more meaningful it becomes. So, I encourage you to make this book your own. That may mean copying down an insight from Joe Renzulli, one of our field's experts, to share with a colleague, or highlighting the equitable access strategy Kurshanna J. Dean used in Maryland schools. Go ahead and mark the pages so that you can apply Minnesota Department of Education's Wendy A. Behrens' advocacy ideas to your own school, district, or state. Better yet, write down and reflect on what brings *you*

DOI: 10.4324/9781003259190-1

joy in this profession, what inspires *you* to continue in this (at times) seemingly impossible pursuit. Actually, you might want to tape that one to your bathroom mirror. That way you're reminded every day the difference you in make in the lives of others.

So settle into your favorite comfy chair with a highlighter in hand and a hot (or cold) beverage by your side. Or, if that's too unrealistic for your crazy schedule, keep the book in your car so that while you're waiting to pick up your daughter from soccer or in a doctor's waiting room with your father, you can peruse a chapter that interests you. Or even tuck it in your desk drawer so that after a particularly challenging class or meeting, you can share in Fred A. Bonner's or Sylvia Rimm's joy for a quick reminder of why you do what you do. Because it's never too late to learn – or relearn – why you are so important to the gifted students in your life, why your work matters.

Contributor and award-winning gifted coordinator April Wells puts your work, this work, into a poetic perspective:

> This work.
> A quest that often reflects a delicate intersection of personal and professional pursuits.
> Our willingness serves to open doors and nurture the beautiful complexities our scholars embody.
> Maintain your resolve.
> This work.
> Espouse a view that allows you to zoom in to see beyond what you may ordinarily apprehend.
> Lift hands who are lifting the work in synch with you.
> This work.
> When you feel you're preaching to the choir just remember, good choirs rehearse.
> Our perspective is shaped by our experiences, and they are as varied as the students we serve.
> Let's galvanize our efforts to make their outcomes greater than our individual names.
> This work.

Reflection Question

What inspires you the most in this profession? Write this down and stick it somewhere you see often; that way you're reminded every day the difference you in make in the lives of others.

2

The Talent Scout

All educators should consider themselves talent scouts, constantly keeping a well-trained eye open for promise, aptitude, ability, creativity, and talent. Some students scream "gifted" when they come to you as stereotypical (and somewhat mythical) Sheldon Coopers or teacher-pleasing, seemingly perfect Hermione Grangers who always turn in homework, earn A's on tests, and run errands for the teacher. Please note that both of these fictional characters are White and middle-to-upper class, speak English as their first language, and come from "traditional" families. But the truth is most gifted students do not look or act like Sheldon or Hermione. In fact, research finds that as many as 3.6 million students from low-income families alone are not identified and served (Seward & Gentry, 2022) – they are *missing*, which is a new measure of access and equity (Gentry et al., 2019). Unsurprisingly, the majority (i.e., 2.2 million) of those missing is non-White. Without the proper training (as the chapter on teacher growth explains), millions of students (and I would argue the future of our nation) are in peril, languishing in mediocrity and not realizing – much less actualizing – potential.

So what can be done about this? First and foremost, everyone in education needs to learn about gifted education and talent development including identifying those learners. The following truths are a strong starting point:

> Eight Universal Truths of Identifying Students for Advanced Academic Interventions (Lee at al., 2020)

> Truth 1: What Is Measured in Identification Must Align With What Is Provided in the Service
> Truth 2: Choose Identification Tools or Protocols That Are Reliable and Valid Measures of the Content and Skills to Be Addressed in the Particular Service
> Truth 3: The Larger the Percentage of Students Formally Evaluated for Gifted Services, the Fewer Will Be Missed
> Truth 4: Do Not Set Arbitrarily High Cut Scores: Criterion for Program Participation Should Have a Rationale Basis
> Truth 5: The Use of National Norms Undermines the Goal of Local Gifted Services
> Truth 6: If Teacher Nominations Are Used, They Should Be Well-Informed and Balanced
> Truth 7: Multiple Measures Are Great, But the Devil Is in the Details
> Truth 8: Be Mindful of Cultural Differences and Potential Biases in Identification and Proactively Mitigate Barriers to Access
> (Lee et al., 2020, pp. 62, 64, 65, 67, 70, 71, 73, 75)

Several of these will be fleshed out in the tips and suggestions that follow. Let's begin with local norms and universal screening as referenced in Truths 5 and 3.

Local Gifted and Talented Expansion: Equity

In 2017, Montgomery County Public Schools introduced local norms in its universal screening process. As a result, students from every elementary school – across racial and socioeconomic groups – were identified for gifted programming. Our team created humanities and mathematics gifted courses for each middle school to address the overwhelming demand for programming. Lesson learned from this endeavor – communicate early and often. Collaborate with your public information team, have them prepare communication tools, and use social media. Work with leadership to get to all parent communities to explain the why and to listen to their concerns and any misconceptions about the work.

Kurshanna J. Dean, award-winning educator with more than two decades of experience in gifted education

Truth 7 focuses on the multiple-criteria process that advocates using varied tools of identification so that no one test or measure (such as a teacher nomination) excludes someone from identification and services. The "detail" refers to using the word *and* instead of *or*, which would make identification even more challenging. No one measure should serve as a gatekeeper. Read on for valuable ideas, beginning with Joe Renzulli's wisdom.

The Birth of a Model

I began my career as a middle school science teacher shortly after the Russians fired Sputnik into space in 1957. Because of this historic event, our superintendent of schools asked me to start an after-school science program for our "gifted students," and he sent me a list of all middle graders with IQs of 130 or higher. Little did I realize at the time that this experience would lead to an examination of two critical issues that in a certain sense have defined my career for half a century.

The first critical issue is who are the gifted and how do we identify them? I did, indeed, begin my special program with the high-IQ students, but because I was a general science teacher, I realized that there were several students in my regular science classes that showed the kinds of interests, strengths, and motivation to learn science that made them excellent candidates for the special program. I started reading everything I could find on gifted education, discovered the concept of creativity, and consumed biographical reading about highly creative and productive people that led me to the concept of "task commitment" in what eventually became The Three Ring Conception of Giftedness model.

Joe Renzulli, one of the 25 most influential psychologists in the world

LJ

Gifted identification protocol should include a multi-criteria process that includes both informal and dynamic assessments (National Association for Gifted Children, 2011 [NAGC]; Renzulli, 2021). Below is an example of a missed opportunity to provide a high-potential diverse student with gifted programming services. LJ is a Black boy in fifth grade who was adopted from Haiti when he was 2 years old. Because of his inquisitive nature and advanced academic performance, LJ was tested in the third grade for the gifted program. Although LJ's nonverbal assessment scores were high, the verbal assessment scores fell below the criteria for placement, so the committee did not review his file. There is no doubt that LJ would benefit from gifted services. Since he was a toddler, LJ has used cardboard boxes and other scraps to make his own toys (such as houses with drawbridges, roller coasters, and musical instruments). LJ enjoys challenges, and he is one of the first students to make connections between concepts. LJ's family is able to provide him with enrichment opportunities to facilitate his learning and talent development. How many students like LJ are not provided with these opportunities at school or home?

Debbie Dailey, associate professor of education and chair of the Department of Teaching and Learning

The Spill-Over Effect

The concept of the spill-over effect *has affected my perceptions of gifted education over the years. The spill-over effect has been the means by which either subtly or deliberately all students within the classroom environment gain access to the differentiated experiences responsive to the attributes and needs of specifically gifted learners. The access provided by the spill-over effect to ALL students also provides the opportunities for students who have not been identified formally as gifted to demonstrate their abilities that may be dormant or go unrecognized. The spill-over effect is a form of nontraditional identification that could unleash the abilities of students that formal or traditional forms of identification fail to identify. The most important aspect of the spill-over effect is that in responding to the needs, abilities, and interests of gifted students, we are responding to all students.*

Sandra N. Kaplan, professor of clinical education and curriculum developer

This next bit of wisdom still addresses Truth 7, but it also refers to Truth 8 sprinkled with a bit of Truth 2. In short, it delivers an important message.

Lesson Learned

Throughout my more than 25-year career in gifted education, I became a stout advocate of mass testing using a nonverbal measure of ability/ intelligence to identify low-income, culturally and linguistically diverse students. For the most part I was successful in identifying Hispanics/ Latinos, African Americans, those who are twice-exceptional, American Indians, and those low-income students attending Title I schools. As a principal, my school often served as a demonstration site for others to visit, observe, and ask questions regarding gifted education. It wasn't until I supervised a mass testing of all students in grades 1–7 in one particular public school district that I learned a very valuable lesson. In this context, all students were racially and culturally diverse. The mass testing accomplished its goal of identifying 42 students who were never considered for gifted education in the past. I, along with my staff and district personnel, were proud of this achievement. However, in taking a deeper dive into the test results, I realized that there were about 10 students in my intermediate school who did not meet eligibility criteria.

It was then that the light bulb went off. These 10 students, who everyone acknowledged were our most academically talented and successful, shared a verbal and linguistic preference/orientation for learning. It was a "duh" moment. After the school psychologist administered a more traditional verbally intensive, language-based test of intelligence, all 10 students met eligibility criteria for gifted education. Lesson learned! That is, despite socioeconomic status, ethnicity, race, and language proficiency, there are students who are low-income and culturally and linguistically diverse who will score higher and meet eligibility status when a more traditional verbal test of ability is administered.

Jaime Castellano, national authority on identification, assessment, recruitment, and retention of low-income, culturally and linguistically different gifted students

Multiple measures and nontraditional assessments prove especially critical when learners are twice-exceptional (2e). Often these students are overlooked altogether, appearing to be average learners in a teacher's eye – their strengths have compensated for their areas of difficulty. Others only have their areas of weakness addressed because difficulties mask the gifts. And some gifted students have other exceptionalities overlooked, with focus only on the gift. Strategies for identifying neurodiverse learners follow.

Stay Curious

It is critical to stay curious with students with disabilities and not overlook their potential for giftedness. Aster is one such student who might have been overlooked. He struggled with written expression but could tell long stories or explicate complex ideas in great detail verbally. Still, when he was given a standardized test, either multiple choice or constructed response, he froze. Luckily his math performance was so exceptional he qualified for gifted services in math, and this later clued us in to his dysgraphia. Had we not recognized he was twice-exceptional, Aster's talents might have been missed or ignored.

Sarah Yost, National Board-certified teacher (NBCT) and elementary school staff developer

Be Aware

It is no secret that students who are twice-exceptional are often under-identified for gifted services as their disabilities may mask their gifts and talents. As a school psychologist, I spend a vast majority of my time completing evaluations for special education purposes and communicating those results with parents and teachers. Unfortunately, many of those conversations tend to center around a student's weaknesses. However, more than once the data have shown that the student is actually twice-exceptional. It is often the first time giftedness has ever been discussed for that student, and, in many cases, it makes previously observed "eccentricities" make sense. It is imperative that school psychologists, or anyone completing these evaluations, be aware of the characteristics of twice-exceptional learners in order to better identify and advocate for each student's individual needs.

Brittany M. Dodds, school psychologist with experience working with twice-exceptional students

When twice-exceptionality is coupled with a multiple language learner, identification becomes even more complex (and ties to Truth 8).

Abdul

As the son of South Sudanese refugees now living in a high-poverty neighborhood where gun violence was a common threat, Abdul was often angry. When I met him, he was in third grade and had just qualified for an IEP for his Emotional Behavior Disorder. His outbursts were sometimes violent and frightening. One day when he was cooling down in my room, I started working with him on some etymology work I had been using with advanced readers. As we dissected the English words and analyzed their Greek and Latin roots, I watched Abdul's face soften and his fists loosen. When I asked if his family spoke Dinka, he brightened and excitedly shared some of what he knew about the etymology of his home language. This was my first tip that Abdul might be neurodiverse, and I was excited to begin assessing him to see if he might qualify for gifted services.

Sarah Yost, public school educator since 2005 and specialist in gifted education

These final tips and suggestions focus on the importance of early identification. Multiple states don't begin formal identification until after primary grades, and these advocates would argue that's not the way to do it.

You Can Teach an Old Dog New Tricks

For years I operated under the assumption that you shouldn't identify giftedness in really young children because their home environment can give them an advantage or disadvantage. Because of this, we didn't identify students until third grade. I took part in a book study that looked at equity and found multiple sources that were contrary to my belief: That the earlier you identify, the more likely you are to catch students who traditionally are underrepresented. It just goes to show that you shouldn't get stuck in your beliefs but rather you should check and recheck the facts.

Todd Stanley, former teacher, gifted coordinator, and author of teacher-education books

Catch Them Early

In Kindergarten, he had a meltdown every week. Other kids didn't understand his vocabulary. His small hands couldn't create the ideas in his mind. He wanted to study the planets, not the letter P. I started working with him that year, providing challenges and guidance on persistence. In first grade, he had a meltdown every other week. In second grade, it was once a month. In third grade, he memorized the Periodic Table of Elements. In high school, he wrote a novel. Today, he is graduating valedictorian and is off to study Computer Science in college. Early identification works.

Tamara Fisher Alley, K-12 gifted education specialist for a school district on an Indian reservation

These nuggets of wisdom bear out many of the truths shared earlier in this chapter but not the first: What Is Measured in Identification Must Align With What Is Provided in the Service (Lee at al., 2020, p. 62). If your state does not support serving students identified as gifted in creativity, then do not identify students in that area. (Do you have them? Of course. But if you can't serve them, it's a disservice to identify, and it is costly, and time consuming.) If your district has nothing in place to advance or enrich students gifted in math such as cluster grouping or subject acceleration, do not identify them. In short, "the content, skills, or dispositions measured by an identification system should align with those fostered in the resulting services" (Lee at al., 2020, p. 62). Examine what services you do offer (or could put into place right away), then identify students for those services. Best practices in identification lead to continuous progress.

Sharing Joy: My Dyslexic Muse

C. Matthew Fugate, professor and researcher who focuses his work on social-emotional needs of twice-exceptional students, culturally responsive teaching, and creativity

One fall day, the 2e student whom I credit as my muse walked into my classroom and told me he was stupid. I was shocked and asked why he would say that. He said that he couldn't read when everyone in the class could. He had dyslexia. I assured him that I saw him as gifted and that we would work on strategies to help him read, but I would only assess him on his understanding of the story. Fast forward to Spring of the following year and my student returned excited to my classroom. He had passed the third-grade state reading test on the first attempt. The look of pure happiness and pride on his face that day is forever burned into my mind.

Sharing Joy: Lucas

Jaime Castellano, co-author of *Identifying and Serving Diverse Gifted Learners: Meeting the Needs of Special Populations in Gifted Education* (2022)

I first met Lucas when he was a 3-year-old Spanish-speaking immigrant from Venezuela. His parents enrolled him in our federal Head Start program. In the beginning, he would yell, scream, hit, kick, and attempt to run away as his parents walked him to his classroom. There were many days when I had to literally peel Lucas off his mother's leg. Eventually, though, he settled in and would greet me each day with a hug and a smile. One year later, Lucas was leading circle time, reading books in English to his classmates, and devouring all the content his Head Start teachers provided. During his kindergarten year in his local public school, Lucas was tested for gifted education services. He was assessed by a bilingual psychologist, that, surprisingly, Lucas himself requested, and he surpassed all the scores needed for eligibility. He is flourishing in his gifted education program and looks forward to what the future brings. This is a story that brings me joy and puts a smile on my face. Si se puede! Yes, we can!

Sharing Joy: I Can't Just List One!

Mary Cay Ricci, author of award-winning, national best sellers on mindset including *Mindsets in the Classroom: Building a Growth Mindset Learning Community*

- When an administrator supported my ideas for equitable access and, as a result, opened the door for many traditionally underserved students.
- When a teacher shares with me the positive differences they have observed in their students as a result of looking beyond test scores, grades, and labels.
- When a child's potential surprises the adults in their life. (Hearing adults say, "I never knew that they could do that.")
- Hearing students explain that their neurons were connecting since they persevered and worked hard.

Reflection Question

How do you currently measure and identify potentially gifted students? After reading this chapter, what changes can you implement to ensure you are reaching and retaining historically underserved gifted students?

References

Gentry, M., Gray, A. G., Whiting, G. W., Maeda, Y., & Pereira, N. (2019). *Access denied/system failure: Gifted education in the United States: Laws, access, equity, and missingness across the country by local, Title I school status, and race*. Report cards, technical reports, and website. Purdue University and Jack Kent Cooke Foundation. www.education.purdue.edu/geri/new-publications/gifted-education-in-the-united-states/

Lee, E. L., Ottwein, J. K., & Peters, S. J. (2020). Eight universal truths of identifying students for advanced academic interventions. In J. H. Robins, J. L. Jolly, F. A. Karnes, & S. M. Bean (Eds.), *Methods and materials for teaching the gifted* (5th ed., pp. 61–80). Prufrock Academic Press.

National Association for Gifted Children [NAGC]. (2011). *Identifying and serving culturally and linguistically diverse gifted students*. www.nagc.org/sites/default/files/Position%20Statement/Identifying%20and%20Serving%20Culturally%20and%20Linguistically.pdf

Renzulli, J. S. (2021). Assessment for learning: The missing element for identifying high potential in low income and minority groups. *Gifted Education International*, *37*(2), 198–208. https://doi.org/10.1177/0261429421998304

Seward, K., & Gentry, M. (2022). Students with gifts, creativity, and talents from low-income families. In J. H. Robins, J. L. Jolly, F. A. Karnes, & S. M. Bean (Eds.), *Methods and materials for teaching the gifted* (5th ed., pp. 343–366). Prufrock Academic Press.

3

Nurturing and Developing Talent

We know quite a bit about serving students with gifts and talents, about methods and practices effective for continuous progress in these exceptional learners. For example, acceleration, in all its various forms, has decades of research proving it to be effective for high-ability students, not just cognitively, but socially and psychologically as well (Assouline et al., 2020). We also know that equity issues must be intentionally addressed in acceleration (Assouline et al., 2020). We understand that when grouping is used effectively (i.e., instruction and curriculum match the reason for grouping), students grow in multiple arenas (Gentry & Cress, 2020). In particular, flexible instructional grouping, cluster grouping, and pull-out programs have shown positive growth (Matthews & Hujar, 2020). Classroom practices such as curriculum compacting and the use of primary sources can lead to continuous growth in learners (Matthews & Hujar, 2020). Problem-based learning (Matthews & Hujar, 2020), inquiry learning (Buerk, 2016), differentiation (Hockett & Doubet, 2020), and independent research (Fisher, 2016) also have strong track records when implemented correctly with gifted learners. Enrichment, both in and out of the classroom, has multiple benefits, from deepening understanding of the content, to connecting students with similar interests (Stephens, 2022).

DOI: 10.4324/9781003259190-3

And, of course, we are deeply aware that one size does not fit all – it's imperative that we offer multiple services in order to address the needs of the varied learners. The following tips, strategies, and nuggets of wisdom should inspire you, as well as challenge you to expand your toolbox.

How Do We Develop Creative/Productive Giftedness?

The launching of Sputnik resulted in my being asked to develop a special program in science for gifted students. I searched the literature curriculum materials for the gifted but found only suggestions for acceleration – teaching advanced material to younger students through traditional instructional procedures. But when I came across a wonderful book by Dr. F. Paul Brandwein, titled The Gifted Student as Future Scientist *(1955), it changed my entire attitude toward teaching. Brandwein advocated (what is popularly being discussed today) the project method and emphasized problem finding and focusing in an area of interest, using instruments of inquiry and thinking skills to gather and analyze data, and producing a product that is targeted to one or more target audiences – exactly what real scientists do when carrying out their work.*

In my teaching I began using a different "brand" of pedagogy that is totally opposite from the deductive, didactic, prescriptive learning used in most classrooms most of the time, and I contrasted lesson-learning giftedness versus creative/productive giftedness. Creative/productive giftedness attempts to create in young people a mindset that is more like that of practicing professionals. Students pursue a topic (in this case in science) thinking, feeling, and doing like practicing professionals (i.e., adult scientists), even if at a more junior level. In later years, this approach resulted in the development of what are now known as The Enrichment Triad Model *(Renzulli, 1976) and* The Schoolwide Enrichment Model *(Reis & Renzulli, 2000).*

Joe Renzulli, leader and pioneer in gifted education and applying the pedagogy of gifted education teaching strategies to all students

In order to provide appropriate services, including The Enrichment Triad Model and The Schoolwide Enrichment Model, we must learn about the students' interests, strengths, readiness, and learning profiles. Preassessment proves critical in matching service (as well as content, process, and product) to learner.

Preassess – Then Act on It

Want to re-engage a challenging gifted learner who has checked out of your classroom or maybe school all together? Determine what they already know and give them credit for it by letting them learn something new and meaningful to them. Want to make your classroom feel smaller? Determine who already knows what you're about to teach. Give the students who already know an independent study or problem-solving activity and focus your instruction on students who really need you. A quick preassessment before each new skill or concept is introduced can save you time, engage your students, and allow you to make a big impact on every student.
Lynette Breedlove, director of a state residential STEM
school for gifted learners

Educators Need to Understand Student Potential

Using preassessments to guide instruction and make adjustments, tailored to meet a student's individual needs, is essential. However, it is important to use more than written preassessments when making instructional decisions. Anecdotal records and your own knowledge of students are also important factors to consider to ensure best practices. Educators should know their students and their potential. Preassessments cannot always show the big picture of how much you are able to extend learning for students. When teachers set high expectations for all students, especially their gifted learners, they will meet and exceed those expectations with teacher support.
Marissa Wilkerson, gifted and talented interventionist
after 15 years of teaching

Show What You Know: Allow a "Boring" Option

My 2e son brings home exciting projects. Make a guillotine using this template. Create a cartoon in these six boxes to explain a concept. He stomps his foot, refuses.

"But you like to build things."

"I printed it out, and it's not sturdy enough, so it won't work. The template is not structurally sound. I won't do it."

"You like drawing."

"The boxes are too small, and I won't be able to draw and write in the boxes, and the teacher won't be able to read my writing because I can't write that small, and I'll fail. I won't do it."

"Why don't you just write what you know, like a normal paper?"

"Not an option."

Angela Novak, assistant professor of education who has served as leadership in both NAGC and TAG

Discovering all you can about the students – from their readiness level in a certain concept to outside interests – affords educators better opportunities to address needs. Listening to the students themselves proves pivotal in the discovery process.

A Place of Learning, Not Loathing

Matthew hated my class as much as the devil hates holy water. To Matt, the work I designed for him was **irrelevant***, a word he wrote boldly in red crayon as he crunched up his assignment, hurling each missive towards my desk. We battled for months. Then I realized something that should have been obvious – I had never asked Matt (or my other students, for that matter) what was important for them to learn. Matt's passion was maple sugar farming (mine was not), and by designing lessons incorporating this topic and finding him a community mentor who had the skills and knowledge I lacked, our classroom became a place of learning, not loathing. Matt's education, and mine, took on new purpose.*

Jim Delisle, author of Gifted Teen Survival Guide *(with Judy Galbraith) and 25 other books*

Jim realized that incorporating student interest into learning impassions students, not simply because they are studying areas of intense interest but also because he valued them as learners and respected them as people. He listened to them. Listening to students, linking standards to interests, and encouraging them to explore self-selected topics empower gifted learners.

Cutting Them Loose

It's simple, really. And yet it sounds terrifying. Giving students the blank-slate freedom to choose, guide, and pursue their own learning objectives and projects . . . ? Was I crazy? Would mass chaos erupt? The opposite happened. I have been happily proven wrong again and again. I knew when I started this job that I had highly capable kids to work with. But until I cut them loose to find and follow their own paths, I didn't truly know just how much they were capable of. . .which is so much more than I, or anyone else, had realized.
Tamara Fisher Alley, award-winning teacher,
K-12 Gifted Education Specialist,
author, blogger, thinker, advocate

Authenticity

Daniel was a third grader when he announced to me that he had suffered from planter warts during the summer and had undergone treatment by his podiatrist. He then explained that warts would be the focus of his independent study project in the GT resource room that year. Following a phone call to his mother who explained that she had pleaded with him to consider other possible topics, I realized I needed to allow my student to pursue his authentic interest.

With support from the kind podiatrist, Daniel spent months in my classroom digging through the doctor's medical school textbooks and pursuing his research. He completed a narrated slide show of a gentleman having planter warts removed and was eager to share his product with other kids throughout the school. When Daniel received only one invitation from his second-grade teacher to share his work, he expressed how disappointed he was. He pointed out that many other kids might experience the anxiety he had undergone when he faced the procedure on his feet. As he spoke, it became clear that he had another idea. He decided to transfer his photographs from the slide show to snapshots and created a book for children in which he assured them that a visit to the podiatrist's office was not something they needed to worry about. He donated his book to the doctor who shared it with others by having it available in the office waiting room. I smiled to myself as I reflected on Dr. Renzulli's insightful message: a child's product addressing a real-world problem and shared with an authentic audience!

Thomas P. Hébert, 2019 recipient of
NAGC's Distinguished Scholar Award

If you've never implemented independent study before, these tips may help.

Independent Study

Independent study projects have long been a critical component of every program model and curricular framework for gifted education. However, they are often challenging for teachers to implement, and students may not find success when their use is haphazard or inconsistent. I have found the most effective independent study projects include three key components: 1) they follow the natural curiosity of the gifted student, not the teacher, 2) assessment emphasizes the learning process, and 3) there must be an authentic audience for the final product. When these three criteria are met, the result is a joyful classroom of students that are truly developing as lifelong learners.

Jessica LaFollette, teacher of gifted students and president of her state gifted association

Learning About the World and Themselves

One important thing that I experienced firsthand while working with gifted individuals was the importance of independent study. Due to a lack of manpower (as a result of Covid), sources for acceleration and

enrichment were scarce; however, I was able to accommodate a very gifted student via independent study. To prepare for this student's independent study, a contract and rubric were made along with many options for independent study within a 2-to-3-week time frame. Each day my student would complete an exit slip for that day's math lesson and would then go to a quiet place of choice with his laptop and have 65 minutes to work. The independent study allowed him to be challenged while I encouraged him to also tap into his creativity. The product of his hard work was a phenomenally advanced math game created solely by this student. Not only did he create a game to be proud of, but it was also used as an artifact in his Backpack Portfolio (a requirement in my district) to reflect how he was an innovative learner. Academically advanced children are naturally curious. Independent studies are critical because they allow students to learn about the world around them while in return learning more about themselves, too.

Patrice Johnson, fourth-grade regular classroom teacher with a gifted and talented endorsement

Remember the importance of respect. Independent study reinforces the concept that students are responsible for their own learning – and that you are there to support in any way possible.

Partners in Learning

Teachers of gifted individuals should never be afraid to treat their students more like partners in learning than subordinates. Promoting regular student input regarding the process and content of activities and projects helps gifted students feel more respected in their education. Having more student input often leads to deeper investment and dedication by students. Furthermore, allowing for student input naturally makes an activity gravitate toward student interests and strengths – an important construct in gifted education. An environment of mutual respect and shared input allows students to take an active role in their instruction and enriches their school experience.

Justin Moreschi, elementary science teacher with specialist degree in gifted education

If you've never provided services for gifted learners, you may want to start by tweaking strategies you already implement.

Critical Thinking Through Open-Endedness

Don't be afraid to teach students who are smarter than you. Don't count yourself short. Intelligent students still have plenty to learn. Spend your time teaching them strategies to identify, process, and analyze problems; finding the answer isn't the objective. Teach them how, not what, to think. Don't ask questions with definitive answers. Ask questions and assign activities with ambiguity. Students will be on the edge of their seats debating and defending their ideas. A finite answer creates an ending to a problem. Remove the ceiling by ending a class without ever coming to a specific answer and watch students experience the "afterburn" of a lesson that endures long after the bell rings.

       Vicki Cooper, *gifted education coordinator of a rural district who has a specialist degree in district-level administration*

Get a Life! Teaching and Learning With Biography

Put a compelling life story into the hands of a child or adolescent and step back. Biography engages and educates through the exciting incident, the telling detail, or the inspiring accomplishment of eminent people who met a challenge and took a chance. Gone are the preachy children's biographies of the early 19th and 20th centuries. Today's children's biographers know a good story when they see one. Teachers can organize instruction around a child or young adult biography through close reading of text, analysis of illustrations, and accompanying creative extensions that encourage talent exploration and identity formation within a talent area (Robinson, 2006). Biographies provide both a mirror to one's talents and a window to the wider world where talents can be explored.

       Ann Robinson, *former NAGC president and editor of* Gifted Child Quarterly, *associate editor for* Gifted and Talented International

That's a Wrap

Creating short films in a middle school gifted classroom is an experience fraught with excitement, tension, and true creative joy. Video is a language that students often speak much better than teachers, but they desperately need practice to plan, execute, and troubleshoot a final product that meets their creative vision. The essential skills of collaboration and compromise are evident from the first day of evaluating student-written screenplays and choosing what to film as a group. Then each day of planning, filming, and editing requires continuous creative problem solving. This curricular strategy can be applied to almost any context and will incorporate strategic thinking into the creative process.

Jessica LaFollette, teacher of gifted students and president of her state gifted association

As we explore tips and strategies for serving learners with gifts and talents, we would be remiss to exclude a strategy that should **not** be used (but often is by well-meaning educators). It is a disservice, not a service.

Gifted Learner as Tutor

Gifted students often grow accustomed to being overlooked by educators due to their advanced ability and most teachers' preoccupation with academic triage for low-ability students. Another common occurrence is teachers assigning their high-ability students as tutors to struggling learners in the classroom. Do not fall into these traps. Tutoring struggling students is not enrichment. Gifted students deserve the same intentionality in enrichment as struggling students deserve in remediation. Take time to learn about the intense interests of the gifted students in your class; students will appreciate your efforts and will feel motivated to demonstrate their gifts and talents.

Felicia M. G. Moreschi, elementary social studies teacher in general education classroom

Acceleration, as mentioned earlier, positively impacts students tremendously (when implemented with fidelity). Read about the difference grade acceleration, one of the 20 types of acceleration, made in Amy's life.

Acceleration Matters

It has been said that thousands of children enter school each fall having already mastered more than half the grade-level curriculum. The prospect of waiting to learn something new is difficult for even the most patient student. At best, these students spend their time daydreaming, helping others, or completing work well below their ability level. They are often disappointed and, at times, disruptive. If given the opportunity for acceleration, these students will find a better match between their instructional needs and the curriculum. When schools implement an acceleration policy, they send a clear message to students. School is indeed a place to learn. The sky is the limit.

Amy lived to read. Early on, she refused playdates, preferring to spend her time alone just reading. Kindergarten was disappointing, and first grade was worse. Amy often cried and, on most days, refused to get on the school bus. When her classroom teacher suggested a special needs assessment, Amy's family agreed. Results confirming Amy's expansive vocabulary, math ability, and verbal fluency led to her first acceleration. With the support of her family and teachers, Amy accelerated twice during elementary school. She found her true peers, made new friends, and graduated from high school at the age of 16. She entered medical school when she was 20. Acceleration saved Amy.

Wendy A. Behrens, gifted education specialist
for her state's department of education advising
educators, families, and policymakers

Wendy mentioned how Amy found her true peers, her people. Gifted students have two sets of peers: their age-mates and their idea-mates. Students need quality time with both. Read about the validation Austin felt when with his true peers.

Intellectual Peers

Austin was the president of the "Save the Animals Club" in an urban elementary school where he served in this capacity as a fifth and sixth grader, organizing his executive board each Friday during lunchtime. With gavel in hand, he led his peers in the gifted program in organizing fundraisers and awareness campaigns for endangered species. My classroom became the headquarters of the club, and I celebrated as Austin's concern for animals became an all-encompassing passion.

At that time, the entire population of the state was emotionally charged as they followed the state university's basketball team to the NCAA championships. My students were animated as they spoke of their favorite players and discussed the statistics of their athletic heroes. A colleague had established a large display of posters and newspaper clippings from the sports page of the state's leading newspaper. When a teacher wanting a photo of the display invited Austin to join his male peers for the photo, the reaction of the young men to Austin's being included was ugly. Austin's lack of athletic ability overshadowed his intellectual gifts in the minds of other sixth graders.

Although Austin may not have held the respect of athletic sixth-grade boys, he was highly regarded by his friends in the gifted program. As the state university's basketball team moved on to championship status, Austin became dedicated to research on endangered animals as his independent project in the gifted program. When his research findings were published in **Creative Kids Magazine** *and he was invited to present his work to a national audience at a summer institute in gifted education, I joined his mother in the auditorium in celebrating his success. It was that evening when I realized just how critical it had been for Austin to join his intellectual peers in a psychologically safe classroom, pursue his passionate interests, and discover his identity as a gifted young man.*

Thomas P. Hébert, professor of gifted education for more than two decades, former teacher of gifted students in K-12 classroom settings

Spending time with idea-mates and interest-mates proves critical in the social and emotional well-being of a child with gifts and talents. Summer programming fits that bill. Kurshanna introduced summer programming for the gifted in her district.

GT Summer Programming

If students cannot access gifted programming beyond the school day, bring the programming to the students. Partnering with colleagues such as the Division of Title I and Early Childhood Programs and Services enabled Montgomery County (MD) Public Schools to implement a federally funded Summer Title I Enrichment Program exclusively for students enrolled in Title I schools. According to Peter Laing, Gifted Education Unit, Arizona Department of Education, "Title 1 funds may be used to provide an intensive summer school course [program] designed to accelerate their [students] knowledge and skills" (personal communication). (To read about the program, go to this website: ww2.montgomeryschoolsmd.org/departments/sharedaccountability/reports).

Kurshanna J. Dean, supervisor of Division of Accelerated and Enriched Instruction for her state

From summer programming to acceleration, independent study to open-endedness, these suggestions have addressed a variety of services. Of course, the goal is matching the service to the learner (and the teacher – you must know how to implement it). Learning about the learner guides us. But we must remember something very important.

Have Fun

When planning lessons, I have a lot of things that I think about, including standards, essential questions, and engagement strategies. One thing that I constantly keep in mind when planning lessons is whether the lesson is fun. I try to come up with activities that are fun for the students and myself. There is no reason why education has to be boring to be challenging. Try to find ways to connect with students that bring laughter and joy into the classroom on a regular basis. If you do this, then students are more likely to want to come to your class and learn because of the enjoyable environment you have created.

Justin Mitchell, National History Teacher of the Year finalist and secretary for his state gifted association

Almost two decades ago, then-NAGC president Del Siegle composed the Gifted Children's Bill of Rights. The second right reads: "You have a right to learn something new every day." Their right becomes your responsibility. Listen closely. Find out as much as you can about the student as well as the service option. Match service to need, strength, readiness, or ability. Read these nuggets of wisdom, internalizing strategies and concepts. Remember, too, the fun of learning and the joy of teaching. It's time to resurrect those concepts.

Sharing Joy: Albert

Sylvia Rimm, internationally known psychologist and author of numerous award-winning books

I've always had an admiration for children who "march to the beat of different drummers." One special joy was Albert in first grade. Instead of doing his workbook writing, he asked the teacher a question about the theory of displacement! I discovered Albert needed full-grade acceleration, and yes, I had to bribe him to complete his written work for a reward (computer programming with a fifth-grade student coach).

Soon Albert became an all-A's student, a terrific soccer player, and a generally nice young man. However, he somehow always found special happiness in the creative edge of every topic. I saw him several times yearly as he pushed his creative envelope.

Albert majored in Physics in college and earned excellent grades. Then his creative edge took over. He earned a master's degree in Photography, traveled the world, and shared his creativity with National Geographic (both on TV and in its journals). What a perfect career for Albert!

My special joy was that Albert and his family stayed in touch. Christmas brought photos of his children and a special one of Albert reading my book *How to Parent So Children Will Learn*.

Sharing Joy: Seth

Debbie Dailey, former high school science and gifted education teacher, current president of The Association for the Gifted, a division of Council for Exceptional Children

When I began teaching in a gifted and talented program nearly 20 years ago, I had a young boy in my class who was very shy and somewhat withdrawn. Seth's home life was different from other boys his age. He lived with his two moms in a small town where this was an anomaly, and Seth was often identified as the boy with two moms. Seth's class met 150 minutes each week with a small group of identified gifted and talented students. Students participated in various curriculum projects, including individual and group research activities, stock market research and games, inquiry-based science units, and various field trips. Seth was in my GT class for four consecutive years, and through that time, Seth became more outspoken, enjoyed digging into cultural projects, and made many new friends. I will never forget his two moms coming to a parent-teacher conference and telling me that the GT program changed Seth's life. He was now eager to go to school, be with his friends, and learn new things. Last I heard, Seth was excelling in a graduate program at Florida State University. The GT program may have changed Seth, but it was Seth who changed me. At that point, I realized the power of community on a shy boy who had few friends; I saw how the excitement of learning is enhanced with experiences and interest-based choices; I learned how vital gifted and talented programs are to the whole child.

Sharing Joy: The Responsibility of Intellect

Michael Postma, founder of Gifted & Thriving, LLC, and father to four children, three of whom are twice-exceptional

One of the pillars of development for gifted students, in my opinion, is developing a positive metacognitive sense of self. In general, gifted students tend to struggle with the *gifted* label and thus never truly understand their potential. So, I put together a project titled The Responsibility of Intellect.

The goals were to have the students engage in a process of learning what it means to be gifted and why having high intellectual potential comes with a responsibility. We began by exploring the idea of giftedness. We deconstructed the term and examined characteristics, definitions, and examples through discussion and debate. I then challenged them to design a community service project wherein they would have to use their intelligence, creativity, and ingenuity to give back in some manner.

Students responded with enthusiasm and vigor. One team, a couple of boys who were passionate about baseball, learned of the poverty-stricken state of the game amongst the youth of Puerto Rico. In the end, they had developed a way to communicate with some youth teams in Puerto Rico, send the equipment, and learn a lifelong lesson in giving. Many other groups created unique projects: blood drives, new school-wide recycling programs, and even outfitting retirement communities with Wii game systems to encourage exercise in retirement communities. However, the greatest achievement was witnessing the change in attitude, self-esteem, and confidence in the students. They had collectively achieved a most important step: They had learned to accept themselves.

Sharing Joy: Joyful Adventures—Place-Based Learning Can Take You Anywhere!

Ann Robinson, distinguished professor at her university and founding director of a leading center for gifted education

Imagine 14 undergraduates from a small-town liberal arts college in the American South spending a term studying in the fizzing metropolis of London. The dramatic shift in location from modern dorm to 18th-century hotel and from grits to beans on toast is a recipe for adventure. What better way to make an unfamiliar world an integral part of learning than to invite students to undertake a passion project of their choice with only one constraint – the project must incorporate London sources and locations into the investigation. What happened? Two students became docents at the Victoria and Albert Museum and took the rest of us on a home and garden tour through the Chinoiserie section of the massive museum. Another student found Hogarth's painting *The Rake's Progress* in the quirky John Soane's Museum and treated the racy material with serious if playful insight. A biology major visited the collections of the great plant taxonomist Carl Linnaeus and received hours of attention from the head librarian who pulled delicate albums of plant samples for her to examine. A nascent playwright studied the stage directions and scene portraits from the Dulwich Picture Gallery to understand how Shakespeare was interpreted by actor David Garrick. Did all the passion projects predict lifelong interests? No, but in at least one case, a student wisely learned what she did not wish to do. Contemplating law school, she sat for weeks at the Old Bailey observing courtroom cases. The experience helped her understand that the life of a legal adversary was not for her. She is now a literature professor in Oklahoma, joyfully specializing in Native American Studies. Place matters.

Reflection Question

In what ways can your existing strategies be tweaked to match the need, strength, readiness, or ability of a variety of learners? Which of the strategies discussed do you feel the most comfortable implementing? The least? Why?

References

Assouline, S. G., Lupowski-Shoplik, A., & Colangelo, A. (2020). Academic acceleration. In J. A. Plucker & C. M. Callahan (Eds.), *Critical issues and practices in gifted education: A survey of current research on giftedness and talent development* (3rd ed., pp. 5–22). Prufrock Academic Press.

Brandwein, P. F. (1955). *The gifted student as future scientist.* Harcourt Brace Jovanovich.

Buerk, S. (2016). Inquiry learning models and gifted education: A curriculum of innovation and possibility. In T. Kettler (Ed.), *Modern curriculum for gifted and advanced academic students* (pp. 129–170). Prufrock Press.

Fisher, T. (2016). Independent research, creative productivity, and personalization of learning: A student-center pedagogy of gifted education. In T. Kettler (Ed.), *Modern curriculum for gifted and advanced academic students* (pp. 171–188). Prufrock Press.

Gentry, M., & Cress, A. (2020). Grouping strategies for use with students with gifts and talents. In J. H. Robins, J. L. Jolly, F. A. Karnes, & S.

M. Bean (Eds.), *Methods and materials for teaching the gifted* (5th ed., pp. 259–278). Prufrock Academic Press.

Hockett, J. A., & Doubet, K. J. (2020). Differentiated instruction. In J. A. Plucker & C. M. Callahan (Eds.), *Critical issues and practices in gifted education: A survey of current research on giftedness and talent* development (3rd ed., pp. 157–168). Prufrock Academic Press.

Matthews, M. S., & Hujar, J. (2020). Using gifted education research in the classroom. In J. H. Robins, J. L. Jolly, F. A. Karnes, & S. M. Bean (Eds.), *Methods and materials for teaching the gifted* (5th ed., pp. 423–437). Prufrock Academic Press.

Reis, S. M., & Renzulli, J. S. (2000). The Schoolwide Enrichment Model: Developing students' creativity and talents. In M. D. Lynch & C. R. Harris (Eds.), *Fostering creativity in children, K-8: Theory and practice* (pp. 15–39). Allyn & Bacon.

Robinson, A. (2006). Blueprints for biography: Differentiating the curriculum for talented readers. *Teaching for High Potential*, 7–8.

Siegle, D. (2007–2009). *The gifted children's bill of rights*. NAGC. www.nagc.org/resources-publications/resources-parents/gifted-childrens-bill-rights

Stephens, K. (2022). Enrichment: In and out of school. In J. L. Roberts, T. F. Inman, & J. H. Robins (Eds.), *Introduction to gifted education* (2nd ed., pp. 201–226). Routledge.

Resources

Danielian, J., Donnelly, U., & Schaff, W. (2021). *The reel classroom: An introduction to film studies and filmmaking*. Routledge.

Matthews, M. S., & Castellano, J. A. (2021). *Talent development for English language learners: Identifying and developing potential*. Routledge.

Powers, E. A. (2008). The use of independent study as a viable differentiation technique for gifted learners in the regular classroom. *Gifted Child Today*, *31*(3), 57–65.

Renzulli, J. S. (1976). The Enrichment Triad Model: A guide for developing defensible programs for the gifted and talented. *Gifted Child Quarterly*, *20*(3), 303–306. https://doi.org/10.1177/001698627602000327

Schlemmer, P., Schlemmer, D., & Pernu, C. (1999). *Challenging projects for creative minds: 12 self-directed enrichment projects that develop and showcase student ability for grades 1–5*. Free Spirit.

Steinke, G., & Zimmerman, J. (2015). *A digital story assignment using mobile devices and WeVideo (a Cloud-Based Video Editing Program)*. Minnesota Summit on Learning & Technology.

4

Breaking Down Equity Barriers

Children with gifts and talents cross all demographics, yet you wouldn't think so when looking at national data. Children who are not Asian or White are two to more than 10 times less likely to be identified (Gentry et al., 2019). In fact, it is estimated that between "2,092,850 and 3,635,533 were missing either because they attended a school that did not identify any children, or because they were a member of a group under-identified in schools that do identify students" (Gentry et al., 2019, p. 4). Unsurprisingly, Black, Latinx, and those from poverty comprise the majority of the missing. The same is true for the excellence gap. Populations struggling in the achievement gap also struggle to attain advanced scoring in national tests, so the gap remains large (Simonsen et al., 2020).

Additionally, not only are students from underrepresented populations typically less likely to be referred for identification by a teacher, but once they are recommended and qualify, some students feel as if they don't belong or feel as if they must choose between their ethnic/racial group and high achievement (Worrell & Dixon, 2020). We know that we must pay attention to the whole child (e.g., cultural and social-emotional aspects), and research tells us this is even more critical with identified students from diverse backgrounds.

Gifted education in the United States has strong roots in prejudice, bias, and ignorance. The inequity inherent in gifted

DOI: 10.4324/9781003259190-4

education and talent development is only part of the problem as Fred A. Bonner II, founding editor of *Journal of Minority Achievement, Creativity and Leadership*, describes:

> If gifted education placement and programming are going to make inroads that will support the success of gifted and talented underserved minority student populations, it is essential to understand what a focus on diversity, equity, inclusion, and belonging in the gifted education contexts truly means. Hence, to say that all student identities are present (diversity), all students have power (equity), and that all students are engaged (inclusion), without a simultaneous effort to ensure that all students feel like they fit in (belong) – we will still continue to see profound disparities in gifted placement and across our gifted education programs.

Julie Gann, NAGC's Gifted Coordinator of the Year in 2021, focuses on the role opportunity and access play in lessening that disparity:

> Providing opportunity and access is key – words I firmly believe and speak into existence daily. Many of our students come to school with such a vast difference to access and opportunity. By educating teachers to become talent scouts and providing access to all students through districtwide procedures, we can begin to chisel away at the barriers and remove the exclusive stigma attached with gifted education. Providing these opportunities can be game changers and change the trajectory of a student's academic journey. Ensuring opportunity and access to each of our students is the most important thing we can do as leaders in gifted education.

As Julie works to ensure equity of access and opportunities in her district, Dina Brulles, former gifted education director in Arizona, has worked to increase inclusion and build equity in gifted education programs and services using culturally responsive practices:

Societal events and disruption to the status quo are beginning to impact gifted education and take hold in our schools. Attention to diversity, equity, and inclusion is now shining a light on the injustices we have experienced in the field of gifted education. Progressive educators are attempting to embrace new approaches for more equitable identification and inclusive gifted programming. Stronger emphasis and energy toward addressing marginalization is impacting how and who we identify and the ways in which we inclusively serve our learners with high ability and high potential. It's about time!

So how do we become change agents in our schools, districts, and states? "Given the diversity of experiences, backgrounds, and opportunities, educators must adopt policies and practices that recognize and value the diversity that their students bring to the classroom" (Wells, 2020, p. 73).

Experts from around the country share their strategies, tips, and ideas on doing just that.

GT Organization Participation and Support

Active participation in local and national gifted organizations grants access to knowledge, resources, and support for innovative, gifted programming. To disrupt the status quo, we collaborated with gifted experts Drs. Joy Lawson Davis, Scott Peters, and Jonathan Plucker to adopt culturally relevant teaching in our magnet programs, refine our universal screening process, and expand gifted programming. Hands down my most rewarding, challenging, personal work to date worth every personal and professional attack from communities that prefer to reserve gifted programming for a select few. It's worth the fight – don't give up! Children are counting on us to get this right! (Interested in learning more? Check out this video: https://mcpsmd.new.swagit.com/videos/28788.)

Kurshanna J. Dean, presidential appointee on NAGC Board of Directors as well as former supervisor of accelerated and enriched instruction

Context Matters

Context matters when structuring schooling experiences that will be both educational and liberating for gifted and talented underrepresented minority learners. I define context *as people, place, and situation. Who are the people (administrators, community, families, role models, staff, and teachers) that contribute in unique ways to how these gifted diverse and underserved learners connect with our classroom, schools, and school systems? What is growth-producing and what is growth-inhibiting about the place (school environment) in which students engage? And what various situations (arts, counseling, testing, gifted and talented programming, sports) do these students find affirming and disaffirming?*

Fred A. Bonner II, endowed chair,
professor, author, and speaker

Developing a context such as Fred mentioned takes intentionality. It requires listening, understanding, and effecting change.

Intentionally Creating Spaces

Simply placing students in gifted programs doesn't guarantee meeting their needs. We must also create spaces where students feel welcome and empowered to contribute to a community. This requires recognizing that some students from marginalized populations feel like outsiders in gifted programs, and many struggle to develop a sense of belonging. Holistically embracing gifted children – in how they think, feel, and learn – means understanding who they are and where they come from, including their culture, family, community and neighborhood, and country of origin. Make students feel welcome and promote voice by honoring, celebrating, and respecting cultural differences by integrating cultural studies into curriculum.

Dina Brulles, author of two NAGC
Books of the Year for practitioners

Equity: Culturally Responsive Teaching

For students of all backgrounds to feel welcome, we must ensure that culturally responsive teaching is integrated into gifted education programs. Our ability to effectively serve all students rests primarily on our level of commitment to being intentional about the ways in which we approach diversity in the classroom. Using tools such as the Bloom-Banks matrix (Trotman Scott, 2014) allows us to go beyond the superficial and think about cultural understanding at a deeper level. When we look at ourselves as educators and consider our own beliefs and biases, we are better able to approach our students and classrooms with an open mind (Fugate et al., 2021).

Jessa Luckey Goudelock, chair of NAGC's
Parent Editorial Content Advisory Board

Relationships Unveil Genius

As an educator and mentor, I have learned the importance of relationships, particularly authenticity in those relationships. Students know whether you genuinely care about them and are encouraging them to succeed in order to help them better themselves from a place of empathy or sympathy. You must believe that the students you work with will be successful, even when they do not. You have to appreciate the assets students bring to the table before you help them grow in less cultivated areas. It is our responsibility to provide students with access to experiences and knowledge to develop their genius.

Stella L. Smith, an assistant professor of
educational leadership and counseling

Instructional leaders should guide their schools, districts, and states by providing professional development opportunities, time, and resources. Change, whether that's through adopting universal screening or implementing the talent development model, occurs when leaders believe the change to be important, so they hold people accountable.

Cultivating Talent Scouts

School principals set the tone for their school's learning culture through what they say and what they do. Their message should be that all staff members are talent scouts, and their role is to find talent. The business of the school should be to develop talent in students. Principals are leaders in talent development when they make sure gifted education is integrated into the general education program, schedule time for services to address strengths, train teachers in the nature and needs of gifted students, and make sure gifted education is a shared responsibility among all the adults in the building.
Mary Evans, former elementary principal
of the year in her state

Talent Development Can Be a Game Changer

The mixture of gifted pedagogy, developing growth mindsets, and an emphasis on talent development can be a strong foundation for more equitable access for historically underrepresented students in gifted education. This shifting from a deficit model, which may be prevalent in public education, to a strength-based model can happen over time. Show people how teaching and learning can happen with engagement and scaffolding for skills and knowledge using high-quality curriculum written for gifted learners. When administrators and teachers see what all students can produce when given support and opportunity, you have a great chance of changing everyday practices in classrooms.
Cheryl McCullough, award-winning gifted services
coordinator for an east-coast district

What does it look like when some of these principles and ideas are set into motion? Here are some possibilities.

Talent Development

This year we decided to start a talent development program for those students who were a little below the cut-off point cognitively for gifted.

We gathered 13–15 third graders at each of our schools and challenged them to think a little differently than they were normally asked to. My biggest epiphany was that parents told me their child was feeling confident in their abilities for the first time. It just goes to show if you let someone know you believe in them, they can begin to believe in themselves.

Todd gathered Stanley, educator, district gifted coordinator, and creator of thegiftedguy.com

Opportunity Matters

Computer science was Mateo's favorite class. Though an English language learner and new to the United States, he excelled at Scratch, the coding curriculum in his third-grade classroom. Mateo's classmates were amazed by the animations and games he created during his free time. Despite his limited English, Mateo and his classmates found ways to communicate and collaborate. Seemingly, against all odds, he became the class leader. Mateo's teacher recognized both his computer science interest and strong math skills. Mateo was recommended for the school's computer science talent development class program where his language and confidence grew exponentially. When we observe and support students, we have the opportunity to change lives. Everything we say and everything we do matters.

Wendy A. Behrens, co-editor of Culturally Responsive Teaching in Gifted Education: Building Cultural Competence and Serving Diverse Student Populations

Engineering a Future With Equity

The recalcitrant effects of poverty on student achievement are not always a hopeless case. Despite the usual research findings that children from low-income households tend to score lower on measures of academic achievement than their more economically advantaged peers, at least one high-powered talent domain differs. Given the opportunity to study engineering (think windmills and plant packages rather than slide rules and differential equations), young children can and do achieve equitable outcomes before and after a modest curricular intervention (Robinson et al., 2018). Why? Perhaps most young children are unfamiliar with engineering and thus begin on a level playing field. Perhaps children who are faced with the constraints of poverty every day have a talent for "making do" within resource constraints – the hallmark of the engineering design process.

Ann Robinson, distinguished professor and founding director of a university gifted center

Celebrating Bilingualism

Culturally sustaining pedagogy emphasizes the need for children to engage actively with their home culture while at school. Effective gifted teaching strategies find ways to honor and celebrate heritage languages. Many project-based learning challenges can be easily tweaked to include a bicultural or bilingual component that values the expertise of children while challenging them to grow their expertise in a heritage language. It is also critical equity work for monolingual peers to begin to recognize and value this skill. For example, in a museum exhibit project, students must offer display signage or audio experiences in multiple languages. During a game design project, rules or cards should be printed in at least three languages. Oral history projects invite extended family members to communicate with students using the heritage language. The best way of all to honor culturally diverse learners is to ask them what types of projects they enjoy, then listen and design learning experiences according to their needs.

Jessica LaFollette, chair-elect of NAGC's Parent, Family, and Community Network

As evidenced by these submissions, some schools, districts, and states are putting great effort into equitable identification and services in the K–12 area. However, it's important that we do not forget the university students. They don't stop being gifted at high school graduation.

The P–20 Spectrum

The success of gifted and talented learners, particularly these high-achieving diverse student cohorts of color who often are underrepresented minority populations in schooling contexts, must consider what minority status means for these individuals across the P–20 education spectrum. The focus on challenges as well as opportunities for gifted diverse learners has to be a process that does not view their engagements with education as divided (i.e., P–12 and Postsecondary), but rather as a seamless experience that allows them to explore and identify aspects of the educational continuum that allow them to focus on assets and potential as opposed to deficits and deficiencies.

Fred A. Bonner II, *endowed chair as well as director of a center focusing on minorities, achievement, creativity, and high ability*

Equally important to the cognitive growth mentioned by Fred is the emotional, psychological, and social growth of the gifted college student. The next chapter focuses on the whole child – here, though, in this next submission, we have the whole person. Gifted adult students need safe venues to process complex emotions and ideas, especially given the climate in America today. Angela made this happen for her students.

Allow Space to Question, to Vent, to Be

In June of 2020, amidst the intersecting pandemics of COVID, racism, and economic insecurity, and shortly after the murder of George Floyd, I posted a discussion board for a summer class of alternative licensure teachers; no grade, no pressure: This optional discussion board is here for anyone who needs to express thoughts or feelings about what's going on right now, and I am here to listen. If anyone wants to ask questions about how to get more engaged with anti-racism work within their classrooms or communities, you can ask questions. *The board exploded with responses from students needing a space to vent and share, questions about how to start equity work, about addressing situations in school, about family, friends. The sharing that occurred was incredibly meaningful for students, and for me.*

> Angela Novak, board member of The Association for the Gifted, a division of the Council for Exceptional Children

Perhaps you've heard the saying "now that you know better, do better." We cannot turn a blind eye to the injustices and barriers facing our children from underrepresented populations. We must stop the systemic racism embedded in gifted education. Take note of the research, strategies, and ideas mentioned in this chapter – many are powerful. What speaks to you? You know better now. It's time to do better.

Sharing Joy: Full Circle Joy – Intergenerational Impact of Equity & Access

Joy Lawson Davis, author of *Empowering Underrepresented Gifted Students: Perspectives From the Field*

One of the sweetest pleasures of doing the work of an equity scholar and advocate is the many lives that I have been fortunate enough to touch over the years. In three decades, I have served in numerous capacities from teacher to district director of gifted services, as a state agency specialist, author, advisor, and professional development trainer. It's the years in these roles that I sometimes take for granted – that is, until I am reminded of the long-term, intergenerational impact of equity activism. A recent incident comes to mind.

Just last fall, I conducted a parent workshop for one of our nation's premier institutions' talent development programs. During the question-and-answer segment at the end of the workshop, a parent spoke up and noted how excited he was to learn from my wisdom during the session, for he had known me for many years: first as an "at-risk" student in a special enrichment program many years ago, and now as a parent. This young man later revealed that I was one of a team of educators that he believed was responsible for the trajectory of his life and for his current-day success. He was humble but proud to share that without the special program, he doubted that he would be "where he is today." The program, he acknowledged, provided the equitable resources, challenging instruction, and support that he needed at a critical time in his life. His participation in the program from his middle school years through high school provided an entry to higher education and a world that students like him would never have participated in. It was the opening of the doors of this program that enabled him to access just the tools he needed to become the highly successful businessman in Fortune 500 companies and now be in a position at one of the nation's most prestigious institutions of higher education. Hearing his voice and listening to his story that afternoon brought me such sheer joy and reminded me of the priceless value of the work that I have devoted my life to for so many years. Now, he acknowledged, I was reaching into his home with my words of wisdom and helping him again, but this time as a parent of a highly gifted Black male child, who is too often overlooked and underestimated in his daily schooling experience.

After that evening, I had to take a pause. I remembered all of the many programs, the students, the parents, the families, the educators who I had interacted with from communities across the nation. The work came alive that evening. Our encounter rejuvenated me. His voice of gratitude made my heart swell with joy. Like so many of you, I see so much tragedy and loss in our world. But hearing stories like this one encourage me to believe again that sometimes it only takes one action to cause a ripple effect that can impact lives across generations. Therefore, we must continue with our efforts to bring equity to all communities as we seek out gifted students across the nation. The right action can create impact intergenerationally and an incomparable joy that may last forever.

Sharing Joy: Our Students Are Our Joy

Angela Novak, presenter at state, national, and international conferences on equity in gifted education

As a university educator, it is not unusual to see my students on *Gifted Child Quarterly* Twitter. I'll invite them if I'm hosting a chat of some kind. One day, someone retweeted a post about an equity commentary and mentioned being my former student. I looked closely thinking, that's not one of my East Carolina University students, must be from University of Virginia, but no. . . . I kept thinking, and I realized: This was a student from a middle school gifted program I taught at more than 15 years ago. And now this student is an educator of the gifted, taking a year off to be a Fulbright scholar. Joy!

Sharing Joy: Hispanic/Latino Parent and Family Bill of Rights

Jaime Castellano, creator of this Bill of Rights, which brings him great joy as he shares it with others

Parents should be aware of not only their responsibilities as advocates but also of their rights as patrons of the school system. This Bill of Rights describes those rights and responsibilities.

Los padres deben ser conscientes de no solo sus responsabilidades como defensores, sino también de sus derechos como patrocinadores del sistema escolar. Para este fin, se presenta una Carta de Derechos para ellos.

Hispanic/Latino Parent and Family Bill of Rights Declaración de los Derechos de los Padres y Familias Hispanas con un Estudiante Dotado/Talentoso Inscrito en las Escuelas Públicas			
	English	Spanish
1	Be communicated with, verbally and in writing, in their heritage language.	Que se le comunique tanto en forma verbal como escrita, en su idioma materno.
2	Be valued and respected as an individual.	Ser valorado y respetado como un individuo.
3	Ask questions and expect answers in a timely manner and in terms that are understandable.	Hacer preguntas y esperar respuestas de manera oportuna y en términos que se puedan comprender.
4	Be part of decision-making that impacts every aspect of their children's education.	Ser parte de la toma de decisiones que impacta todos los aspectos de la educación de su hijo.
5	Expect a world-class education for their children, including access to a curriculum that is rigorous and responsive to individual needs, interests, and talents.	Esperar una educación de clase mundial para sus hijos, incluido el acceso a un plan de estudios que sea riguroso y responda a las necesidades, intereses y talentos individuales.
6	Visit the child's school and classroom at any time.	Visite la escuela y el salón de clases del niño en cualquier momento.
7	Evaluate the effectiveness and responsiveness to issues that impact their children.	Evaluar la eficacia y receptividad de los asuntos que impactan a su hijo.

8	Expect when there are issues related to their child's academic, social, or emotional and mental health development that concerns will be taken seriously and appropriate services will be implemented in a timely manner.	Espere que cuando haya problemas relacionados con el desarrollo académico, social o emocional y de salud mental de su hijo que se tomen en serio y se implementen los servicios apropiados de manera oportuna.
9	Have their children receive gifted education services in their home, school, and community.	Hacer que sus hijos reciban servicios de educación para superdotados en su escuela y comunidad de origen.
10	Expect their child will be taught by a highly qualified teacher.	Contar con un maestro altamente calificado y atento que le enseñe a su hijo.

Reflection Question

Which of the research, strategies, and ideas mentioned in this chapter appeals to you? How can you incorporate it into your practice?

References

Fugate, C. M., Behrens, W. A., Boswell, C., & Davis, J. L. (Eds.). (2021). *Culturally responsive teaching in gifted education: Building cultural competence and serving diverse student populations*. Routledge. https://doi.org/10.4324/9781003234029

Gentry, M., Gray, A., Whiting, G. W., Maeda, Y., & Pereira, N. (2019). *System failure/access denied. Gifted education in the United States: Laws, access, equity and missingness across the county by locale, Title I school status, and race*. Executive Summary. www.dropbox.com/s/d6u13umiv7a8i6y/Access%20Denied%20Executive%20Summary.pdf

Robinson, A., Adelson, J. L., Kidd, K., & Cunningham, C. M. (2018). A talent for tinkering: Developing talents in children from low-income households through engineering curriculum. *Gifted Child Quarterly, 62*(1), 130–144. https://doi.org/10.1171/0016986217738049

Simonsen, M. A., Peters, S. J., & Plucker, J. A. (2020). Excellence gaps. In J. A. Plucker & C. M. Callahan (Eds.), *Critical issues and practices in gifted education: A survey of current research on giftedness and talent development* (3rd ed., pp. 201–212). Prufrock Academic Press.

Trotman Scott, M. (2014). Using the Blooms–Banks matrix to develop multicultural differentiated lessons for gifted students. *Gifted Child Today, 37*(3), 163–168. https://doi.org/10.1177/1076217514532275

Wells, A. (2020). *Achieving equity in gifted programming: Dismantling barriers and tapping potential*. Taylor & Francis.

Worrell, F. F., & Dixon, D. D. (2020). Diversity and gifted education. In J. A. Plucker & C. M. Callahan (Eds.), *Critical issues and practices in gifted education: A survey of current research on giftedness and talent development* (3rd ed., pp. 169–184). Prufrock Academic Press.

5

The Whole Gifted Child

Have you ever heard the adage "if you know one gifted child, you know one gifted child"? It's so true. No two are the same. And when it comes to multiple exceptionalities such as a gifted learner who is multilingual, an autistic child gifted in math, or a gifted student from an impoverished background, those differences are magnified. The cognitive needs of a potentially talented Kindergartner from a home with no print materials varies greatly from a potentially talented Kindergartner whose home is rich with resources. So, of course, needs of young people with gifts and talents may very well differ from those without gifts and talents. Just as the emotional needs of gifted learners can differ from those needs of fellow students, so can the emotional needs differ from one gifted child to the next. In fact, psychological, physical, social, and cognitive needs in addition to emotional ones should be taken into account when educating and parenting gifted learners. We must consider the whole child.

This is exactly what then-president of the National Association for Gifted Children (NAGC) George Betts (2016) did during his term. He created The Whole Gifted Child Task Force in 2018. This important task force ultimately produced a document emphasizing the need to understand the gifted child as a complete, individual human so that we can better nurture and address their needs. Here are some of the takeaways from the report:

- Focusing strictly on academic achievement or talent development can draw our attention away from considering the encompassing learning needs of the whole child
- Enfranchising the whole gifted child requires that we look beyond a child's performance and instead look at the unique characteristics that enable him or her to leverage efforts toward achieving well-being, a state of being which may or may not, be centered around the talent
- When gifted children feel understood, accepted, and appreciated for who they are, not solely for what they can do at the time, children are more likely to take academic risks, accept academic challenges, and feel confident with their efforts
- Building self-esteem within gifted children opens endless opportunities, which is critically important for children who come from populations that are typically underrepresented in gifted education and talent development programs. Doing so embraces, enfranchises, and empowers gifted students from all populations

(The Whole Gifted Child Task Force, 2018, p. 12)

So how do we – critical stakeholders in the development of gifted learners – incorporate these in our work? This report goes on to include recommendations and resources, all worthy of consideration.

Messaging is also an important consideration. Fred A. Bonner II, a scholar who specializes in the journey of gifted Black males, emphasizes the importance of positive messaging from an early age:

The most valuable lesson that I learned during my formative years, gleaned from the teachings shared by my grandmother, was that being a "whole" person was probably the most key aspect of my learning, growth, and development. Her saying was, "If you arrive in pieces, you might not depart whole." What I inferred from her words of wisdom was that I am the sum-total of who I was as an individual, and how I chose to show up in the world – young, gifted, talented, Black, and male – that each one of these identity vectors made me who I was.

Fred's colleague, assistant professor Stella L. Smith, focuses on the importance of seeing the whole student:

Particularly for marginalized students, you must see the whole student. All students have intersectional identities, and it is important to acknowledge the varied lived experiences and positionalities of the students that we serve. Their identity makes them who they are. It must be valued and acknowledged. As educators, we have to put in the work to learn about our students and unlearn our own implicit bias. When you embrace learning and understanding the whole student and see them through an intersectional lens, you are able to help them unleash their untapped potential.

In agreement, psychologist and prolific author Tracy L. Cross zeroes in on students as individual people or whole persons:

Schools are primarily a social enterprise where, on a good day, some academic learning takes place. With that comment, I am reflecting on my decade of overseeing a residential high school for intellectually gifted students, conducting phenomenological research on the lived experience of students with gifts and talents, and having raised four gifted children. The core of this advice is rooted in the realization that no two gifted students are the same, and each has their own set of lived experiences. In short, it means that each of the students we serve is unique, with idiosyncratic natures and needs. One size cannot fit all.

So what can we do to address the whole child in gifted education? Here are some ideas and strategies from various experts in the field. To begin, we must establish school and classroom cultures that encourage individuality and support all aspects of the child.

Classroom Culture

Gifted children need to know that when they step into your classroom, they have entered a space in which they are intellectually, socially, and emotionally safe. They deserve to feel seen, understood, and validated. This can be accomplished by listening, encouraging, and respecting them. The most impactful teachers are the ones who give their students space to be their true selves without fear of judgement or unrealistic expectations. They value their students as individuals with unique perspectives, complex emotions, and unseen struggles. These teachers joyfully invest in their gifted students to encourage total realization of their potential.

Felicia M. G. Moreschi, gifted endorsed
elementary classroom teacher

Ask, Listen, and Respond/Act

If you want to know what students are thinking, feeling, or what they know . . . ask! Often, teachers are looking for a hidden way to find information, seeking to be the Sherlock of 221B. Dr. Asa Hilliard said there is no mystery in how to teach children; you treat them like human beings and love them. Talk to students about what they are learning, what is going on – in class, in life – and how they are feeling. Actively listen. If possible, make changes in your learning environment or curriculum; if not, provide a thoughtful response from an authentic frame of "it's not my classroom, it's ours."

Angela Novak, co-chair of National Association for
Gifted Children's Diversity and Equity Committee

A Balance

Find the balance between leading and guiding. Gifted students need educators who understand both their academic and social-emotional needs – educators who will work to find appropriate content to stretch their thinking and learning. However, my experiences have also led me to see that gifted students often yearn for their own ideas, thoughts, and interests to be validated. Providing students the space, resources, and support to pursue their interests and passions is an essential part of gifted education. When we are able to provide these spaces, it gives our students a mental and physical outlet to explore and learn in innovative and creative ways.
Jessa Luckey Goudelock, gifted program director in the Midwest and recipient of the 2019 NAGC Carolyn Callahan Doctoral Student Award

Knowing how to design such a space should have its roots in teacher education programs.

Teacher Candidates

My time teaching in a gifted and talented program was one of the most rewarding teaching experiences in my career. Seeing a child's love for learning grow by giving them opportunities to explore their interests, develop their talents, and engage in new and unique experiences changed my overall teaching practices. As I moved to higher education, I still try to provide these opportunities for my teacher candidates and encourage them to use a pedagogical approach focused on student-centered learning that addresses the whole child. These include strategies to get to know each student and provide multiple modes of learning through representation, expression, and engagement (CAST, 2022).
Debbie Dailey, former high school science teacher and gifted education teacher, current professor of education

Yes, it's critical that teacher education students learn about talent development and teaching children with gifts and talents. In order to focus on assets and potential, we must know our students well.

Opportunities to Learn

Many opportunities exist for teachers to learn more about their students. Getting to know a student's family, extracurricular activities, and other endeavors help create a stronger portrait of a student's strengths and interests. Taking the initiative to learn more about a student or attend events in their life outside of school stimulates a better relationship between school and home. Attending games, recitals, or celebrations shows a student and their family that a teacher is invested in that student's education and emotional well-being while offering insight into a student's strengths and interests.

Justin Moreschi, fourth-grade science teacher who is certified in special education and endorsed in gifted education

Remember Your Why

I was the weird kid with crazy ideas who saw everything much differently than others. Scattered and unorganized, I was almost 40 until I was comfortable in my own skin. Kevin was bored in English class and kept his head down but aced the tests. He didn't care what I knew, until he knew I cared about him specifically. Although Kevin was brilliant, his behavior was challenging. Autism presented unique obstacles he had difficulty managing. Strive to assure each student can navigate the trenches their gifts present. Every person has a place; helping each student find theirs is mine.

Vicki Cooper, education specialist in a rural school district in the south

School changed for Kevin once he realized his teacher really cared and that she was going to teach to his strengths. As to twice- or multiple-exceptionalities, Kevin was neurodiverse in two ways: gifted in language arts and autistic. Neurodiverse learners bring great value to classrooms once they are encouraged and celebrated for who they are.

Neurodiversity

My mentor used to always remind me that what a society values, it supports. I'm always excited when I see that support for all neurodiverse learners, including gifted and 2e learners, in schools and the larger world outside. When administrators and school-based professionals embrace the special educational, social, and emotional needs of these learners, I see that value and, more importantly, the students feel valued and supported. When each student feels their value, that meets a basic need, which sets the stage for deeper exploration, personal growth, and development. Neurodiversity brings so much to a classroom or a work environment – embrace it, value it, support it, and provide the space for gifted learners to thrive!
Edward R. Amend, director emeritus of Supporting
Emotional Needs of the Gifted (SENG)

Exceptional in Multiple Ways

Visit the stationery section of Target, and you may see what Josh has been creating. He is a successful graphic designer with his own company. Josh had strong math ability, created detailed drawings, and had an insatiable curiosity for learning, but he struggled greatly in reading. He was also an excellent swimmer who traveled to compete in swim meets. His mother shared that he never worried about his swimming performance, but he was very worried about where the bus would stop for lunch. He was so relieved when lunch was at McDonald's because he would not be embarrassed at his inability to read the menu. That anecdote describes the frustration and humiliation that 2e students face every day and why their gifts must be addressed along with their disabilities.
Mary Evans, former state elementary principal of the
year and current program developer at a university center for gifted education

Misdiagnosis/Neurodiversity

Think broadly about what every individual is capable of accomplishing. Through neuropsychological research, we know our historical and conventional notions of brain anatomy and function are lacking. The increasing evidence of the vast neurodiversity among students with gifts and talents means education must be responsive and flexible to meet their needs. The labels we have used to conveniently sort and frame our students historically, including by age, will need to be things of the past for the immense potential of these students to be developed. A school-based talent development model that utilizes our most effective practices in gifted education can help all students maximize their potential.

Tracy L. Cross, executive director of both a center for gifted studies at a university as well as an institute charged with researching suicide of gifted students

An Understanding

I was teaching at a public high school for gifted students in South Carolina when I had a call from my principal – a mom of one of my ninth graders wanted to meet with me. "Odd," I thought, "I've only taught her son for two days." She was nervous as she began speaking, then thanked me. Here's why: I had shared an essay written by a teenager on being twice-exceptional, a term my student had never heard. In the essay, her son had found himself. Two years later, Andy and I still meet monthly, so he can share his self-revelations with me over lunch.

Jim Delisle, worldwide consultant on issues related to gifted students' social and emotional growth

Three Things

Author*Tom Bodett once said, "They say a person needs just three things to be truly happy in this world: someone to love, something to do, and something to hope for." In my years of working with 2e students, this is a message that I have not only kept front and center in my mind, but one that I try to convey to my students: maintain high expectations – you will meet them, honor your strengths in everything that you do and make those a central part of your learning experiences, and celebrate every success. In doing so, I share a message of love and respect.

C. Matthew Fugate, former elementary teacher and gifted coordinator, current professor

* *paraphrase of G. W. Burnap (1848, p. 99)*

Indeed, both strengths and challenges (including those in the social-emotional realm) need to be addressed by educators and families. It's your job to realize these specific needs exist and know the best ways to approach them.

Remember Who They Are

Remember they are gifted. They are exposed every day to tragedy and joy and everything in between – while likely understanding the implications of these experiences. Be a rock and be available to gifted students as they perceive the realities of life much more realistically than we may want based on their chronological age. Yes, they are gifted, but they are also children, students who are developing and need the support and space to express what they are seeing, perceiving, and feeling so that they can respond and contribute in a healthful way.

Megan Parker Peters, psychologist who works primarily with gifted and 2e learners and who has held leadership positions in her state and national gifted associations

Coping With Competition: The Secret to Achievement

The ability to persevere in competition is central to achievement. Educators should teach children how to cope with competition because developing resilience is synonymous with achieving in life. Children can learn to creatively view their failures and losses as learning experiences. They can identify problems, remedy deficiencies, reset goals, and grow from their experiences. Failures should be viewed as temporary setbacks. They can learn to attribute their failures to lack of effort, unusual difficulty, or the extraordinary skill of other competitors. As coping strategies, they can laugh at their errors, determine to work harder, and/or redesign their achievement goals. Most importantly, they should see themselves as falling short of a goal, not falling short as people. Effort counts!

Sylvia Rimm, international presenter, prolific writer, and psychologist who founded an achievement clinic

Build Conceptual Understanding

I remember visiting a classroom to facilitate experiences that helped children learn about the importance of perseverance, resiliency, and working hard (growth mindset thinking). At the end of the learning experience, I asked the children to share with me something that they learned. One little guy enthusiastically raised his hand and said, "We need to put forth effort!" I agreed with him, and, not a moment later, he raised his hand again and asked, "What's effort?" What I realized at that moment is that we must spend time building conceptual understanding of the concepts that we are teaching. What are some examples? Non-examples? Concrete and abstract illustrations of the concept? Students from all backgrounds will be more prepared to apply thinking to a variety of situations if they develop a conceptual understanding.

Mary Cay Ricci, former teacher and district instructional specialist, current consultant and award-winning author

Guiding Fearful Anxious Children

Most children experience some fears and anxiety, although some experience more than others. Fears take place when children are exposed to something that they don't understand or feel they can't control. A sympathetic explanation, a light on, a door left open, or a comforting hug is sufficient to allay these fears for many. Some children, however, seem to remain fearful and overanxious. If adults use negative and threatening approaches, children become more anxious. Overprotecting them and overtalking their fears with them typically only increase their fears. Counterintuitively, adults can be positively assertive and help children take small steps of courage. When adults praise their courage, they gradually become more confident and make positive adjustments to their anxieties.

Sylvia Rimm, former regular contributor to NBC's Today Show *and host to public radio's* Family Talk

Help for Dysregulation

As a school psychologist, I have seen an increase in referrals for students experiencing emotional and behavioral dysregulation in the past year. This has included gifted students who possess overexcitabilities or emotional intensities. When this happens, I do my best to educate not only the adults on how overexcitabilities can present in gifted students, but to also help the students identify and name their own emotions and intensities. I have found that The Gifted Kids Workbook: Mindfulness Skills to Help Children Reduce Stress, Balance Emotions, and Build Confidence *(Boorman, 2018) is a fantastic resource in helping guide students through this process. It includes 27 worksheets for students to complete independently or with the assistance of a counselor, parent, or teacher. I highly recommend this workbook!*

Brittany M. Dodds, public school psychologist and adjunct instructor

Social Support from Gifted Peers

One of the most magical aspects of a great gifted classroom is that it is a safe place to experience both success and failure. When gifted learners are working hard with intellectual peers for long enough, they will undoubtedly experience both. Teaching children to recognize these moments in each other and empathize is one of the most valuable lessons a gifted educator can offer. This requires modeling, coaching, and reinforcement to be effective, but it is incredibly powerful. Schedule times for small groups to intentionally discuss something they are proud of and something they are challenged by. Then coach them to offer encouragement and appropriate advice to each other. This group can provide a true safety net for them as they realize everyone faces challenges.

Jessica LaFollette, teacher of gifted and talented students for more than two decades

The Power of Adult Talk

Discussion among adults about children or about the daily news may have an even more powerful effect on children's feelings and behaviors than direct praise or negative comments. The term referential speaking *describes conversations that take place between parents and others, and yes, even among teachers – all within the children's hearing. Referential talk is often everyday talk by persons who may not have the time to speak confidentially with others, and, thus, they describe children to other adults without thinking about the impact on those children. Too high or spectacular praise mixes extreme pressure with delight. Worried comments about children or the world incur fear and anxiety. STOP – Think! Children may be listening.*

Sylvia Rimm, psychologist who directs
an achievement clinic and prolific author

Social and Emotional Learning and Academic Development Are Not Separate

Social and emotional learning (SEL) has garnered great attention in recent years, but it is often treated as a separate element to address in the classroom or school. When discussing differentiation strategies, we focus on the academic impact they make for students. For gifted and talented students, these are not separate elements. Appropriate differentiation meets students' social and emotional needs at the same time it addresses their academic needs. Self-regulation and interpersonal skills facilitate academic development. Each time we try a new strategy, whether coming initially from an academic or SEL perspective, we need to consider how it impacts all parts of students' development.

Lynette Breedlove, former president of TAG
(a division of CEC) and two state gifted organizations

Empowerment

I believe that gifted students need to be instructed on how to navigate their giftedness in relation to their social and emotional needs. When students are exposed to instruction that is individualized to their specific talents, they need to know how to deal with the shift in instruction, so they know what to expect. I have had several gifted students over the years, and one thing they struggle with is making mistakes and perfectionism. Teachers and parents need to work together to give students the correct tools to overcome some of the psychosocial characteristics that come with being more advanced than their peers of the same age level.

Marissa Wilkerson, gifted and talented
interventionist at an urban elementary school

As educators and family members, we can't simply extract one aspect of a gifted learner as our focus. These children are complex humans who differ from typical learners as well as each other. More importantly, we shouldn't fixate on nurturing and developing the *gift* of the learner; rather, our focus should be on the *learner* who happens to be gifted or neurodivergent. Watch what happens when you prioritize the *whole child*: I guarantee it will surpass your expectations!

Sharing Joy: What We Say Matters

Wendy A. Behrens, president-elect of The Association for the Gifted (TAG)

Words matter. They convey our thoughts, our emotions, and may serve to motivate or empower our students. When used carelessly, they can be hurtful or even devastating. From people who use them well, they can offer a port in a storm, a safe harbor for a student in need of affirmation or encouragement. Some of my best words have been unspoken, a reassuring smile or a nod signaling support in difficult times. My best-spoken words have been used to provide hope or an honest appraisal in advocacy for students. Words matter.

Kai sat near the door, as if he might need a quick escape. He waited nervously for math team practice to begin. A head taller than most, he wore his hair neatly braided and clothes that were clean but well-worn. I startled him saying, "Kai, I'm glad you came today." When we divided into smaller practice teams, he looked at me, as if to say, "I can't do this." Kai's team won the competition that day, earning suckers as "trophies." Kai stayed in the room after practice. Staring at his sucker, he said to me, "I've never won a prize in school before. I really can do math, can't I?" I followed by saying, "Of course you can!" and so, he did.

After experiencing success, Kai discovered a love for learning. His attendance and grades improved overall. He'd stop by my office to say hello, share a joke, or tell me something he found interesting. I lost track of Kai that fall when he entered middle school. Years later, standing in line at the grocery store, I heard someone say, "See that lady? She told Daddy he was good at math." I turned to see Kai holding the hand of a little boy. His hair was still braided, now with pressed clothes, wearing a collared shirt and tie. I later learned he became a math instructor at our local technical college. For Kai and for me, words made all the difference.

Sharing Joy: Life Itself

Tracy L. Cross, author of more than 200 articles, book chapters, and columns; presenter of more than 300 presentations at conferences; and writer of 14 books

A few years ago, I was contacted by a gifted adolescent male who wanted to talk with me before he killed himself. He thought it might help others to learn of his experience.

He wrote anonymously about his plans. I had three intense emails with him, eliciting bits of information. With little to go on, my wife and I were able to determine his location and a possible school. We sent emails to four school employees and waited. Thirty minutes later, we heard from one of them that he was their student. They contacted local police who immediately went to the boy's home and confiscated his gun. His parents had no idea of any of this. The boy spent some time receiving services and is alive today. When his mother contacted me to thank us, I have never felt so much joy. All the hard work of several people fell into place and helped to save this boy's life.

Sharing Joy: Molly's Story

Thomas P. Hébert, award-winning author of books including *Guiding Gifted Students With Engaging Books: A Teacher's Guide to Social-Emotional Learning Through Reading and Reflection*

Molly had an effervescent smile and freckles. As a student in my middle school gifted education seminar in Bad Kreuznach, Germany, she was enthusiastic about learning, intellectually curious, highly motivated, and managed to avoid the daily teenage drama prevalent amongst seventh and eighth graders. As a teacher in the Department of Defense Dependents Schools (DODDS), I learned how children of military families were resilient as they negotiated their transient way of life. I saw that these kids were quite remarkable, and I thought Molly was pretty special. As I taught these young people and we traveled the continent on field trips together, I learned to appreciate the sacrifices they made as their parents served their country and fulfilled their military obligations.

> I left Bad Kreuznach and moved on to a career in higher education. As a university professor I was delighted to return to Maine, my home state, to deliver a keynote address at the annual conference of gifted education teachers. Just minutes before I was to deliver my speech, I noticed a short red-headed young woman approach the podium to provide my introduction. A well-respected teacher of gifted kids in Maine, she told her story of being a DODDS student and shared her experiences of being a student in my classroom. She highlighted the adventures we had experienced on European field trips. She pointed out to the audience that although they might know me as "Dr. Hébert, the author of all of those research articles, I will always know him as Mr. Hébert, the teacher who took me and my friends to London and Budapest." Hugs, tears, and laughter happened at the podium and provided me with joyful energy to deliver an inspirational keynote!

Sharing Joy: Small Town Moments

Tamara Fisher Alley, author of "Unwrapping the Gifted" for NAGC's *Teaching for High Potential*

"Ms. Fish, do I get a prize for solving this puzzle?"

"Prove you solved it first."

He lays the nine pieces on the table. It is solved, but I don't recognize the puzzle he is returning. I have puzzles like it, but this one is not familiar. Yet there is "GT" in my handwriting written on the corner of the packaging. It dawns on me . . . His mother – one of my former students – checked out the puzzle almost two decades earlier and never returned it! Here was her son, a third grader, returning it. They had solved it together. Two prizes!

Sharing Joy: Personal Inroads

Patrice Johnson, parent of gifted girls who inspired her to get her gifted education endorsement

Some gifted characteristics can be extremely challenging when trying to teach a diverse class of learners in today's society. Characteristics such as psychomotor, intellectual, and emotional overexcitabilities or intensities can make for interesting moments within the classroom. However, encounters with such students are also advantageous. I found that creating personal inroads and rapport with students, educating myself more about gifted and talented learners, and having patience make a difference for all learners. I will never forget one particular friend that challenged me from the first day I "met" him online. Because I sought to know him beyond his exceptionalities and allowed him to know me as a person (aside from being his teacher), we developed a bond that has lasted since. He even taught me how to play chess. I must confess that I am still not very good at it but watching the joy on his face as he taught me various moves remains one of my fondest memories as a teacher. I will never forget my friend, and I suspect he will never forget me.

Sharing Joy: Spend Time with Kids

Todd Stanley, gifted coordinator and author of books including *Project-Based Learning for Gifted Students (2nd edition)* and *Promoting Rigor Through Higher-Level Questioning*

If you want to have joy, you need to be spending more time with children than with adults. I have been in administration for the past 7 years, but I have always made efforts to continue to work with kids whether it be enrichment opportunities, online tutoring, or academic extra-curriculars. I find my stress level on days I'm mostly working with adults is much higher and the days I am working with children to be far more satisfying. If you are someone in administration who is having a bad day, walk into a classroom and work with kids. It will bring you much joy.

Sharing Joy: Student Contact

Brittany M. Dodds, school psychologist and presenter at national and international conferences on gifted education

During my school psychology internship, one of my amazing advisors, Dr. Charles Barrett, told us: "A day without student contact is a day wasted." As school psychologists, it is so very easy for us to spend days holed up in our offices trying to get caught up on reports and other due process paperwork. However, when I reflect on the moments this past school year that have brought me joy, they have all involved working directly with students. I have laughed with students, cried with students, commiserated with students, cooked with students, and played with students, and I would not trade those moments for all the report writing time in the world.

Sharing Joy: Watching Giftedness at Work

Felicia M. G. Moreschi, elementary social studies teacher with a specialist degree in gifted education

My fifth-grade class was researching monarch butterflies. One of my students wanted to know if butterflies preferred a certain sugar level in the nectar they drink. My student and I worked together to find an answer and discovered that butterflies prefer lower amounts of sugar in nectar, while pollinators like hummingbirds prefer higher concentrations. My student hypothesized (correctly) that this must be because hummingbirds expend more energy than butterflies and flap their wings much faster than butterflies. He discussed how butterflies do not regulate their body temperature, unlike hummingbirds. He even considered that the proboscis on a butterfly is different from a hummingbird's beak, which might contribute to the nectar preferences of these animals. I felt energized by his hyper-focus, extreme desire for answers, and rapid-fire brainstorming of ideas. I watched giftedness at work right before my eyes. His ability for such deep analytical thinking and processing of complex information was fascinating to me.

Sharing Joy: The Ripple Effect

Edward R. Amend, clinical psychologist who has held various leadership roles with NAGC, SENG, and *The G WORD* film's advisory board

Recently, I was contacted by the proud parent of a first-year college student who shared the joy of sending their son, whom I had evaluated years prior, off to college. When we met, he was struggling not just to learn but simply to be in a world he didn't understand and one he felt didn't understand him. This mother described the hope that came from the evaluation and how both she and her son were better able to make sense of themselves and their world. As a psychologist, I meet many people on their personal journeys toward a better self. Often, these encounters include only a few sessions of evaluation, consultation, or therapy. I may provide information, direction, guidance, or simply reflections. With such limited contact, I am often left wondering about our impact. Hopefully, I've helped them set a positive path forward. My sense of purpose is renewed each time I see or hear about an accomplishment of a former client, or when a new client comes in having been referred by a past client. I am especially touched and humbled when a client I saw many years before asks to come back for a "tune up" session or two. Knowing they still have trust in me after so many years motivates me to keep going. As a grownup gifted kid, I feel pride knowing I'm making a small difference and hope it ripples. But, remember, even when we don't hear anything, no news may indeed be good news so please stay positive about the impact you make every day!

Sharing Joy: An Independent Project

Justin Moreschi, elementary science teacher with degrees in elementary, special, and gifted education

I always offer opportunities for independent practice. Years ago, after teaching a unit on electromagnetism, a student asked if she was allowed to make electromagnetic shoes for her independent project. Initially, she had hoped she would be able to walk up a steel I-beam but settled for picking up copious amounts of purposefully spilled paperclips in her presentation to the class. Her electromagnetic shoes were expertly planned with independent switches for each foot attached to her belt for easy access. She presented her creation to the class by creating a man-on-the street style performance for her classmates. This was the first clear example of giftedness I remember witnessing in my classroom.

Sharing Joy: Student Love

Justin Mitchell, chair of his state's Education Professional Standards Board

Seeing my students successful is what brings great joy to me and keeps me wanting to teach. My favorite thing that my school district does is a Senior Walk, where graduating seniors walk around to all of their former schools dressed in their graduation caps and gowns. Students are allowed to give out honorary diplomas to teachers that have made a difference in their lives, and these are some of my most treasured gifts. I love all the hugs, handshakes, and thank yous that I receive that day. It is something that keeps me going as a teacher.

Sharing Joy: A Slice of Pie

Vicki Cooper, teacher, advocate, and district coordinator

One afternoon, I was reading through essays a student asked me to revise for his application to a prestigious alternative high school. My eyes filled with tears while reading the one about overcoming adversity. He shared his experience of not fitting in at his new school and the agony it brought him. He wrote about his first day coming to my gifted class: "Everyone was like me, even the teacher was weird, but in a good way. . . . That class saved my life." He explained the impact my class had made on his life. Don't discount your ability to make a difference.

Sharing Joy: Keeping Connected

Lynette Breedlove, educator, parent, administrator, leader, and advocate

As a gifted and talented specialist, I often had the opportunity to work with students several years in a row as they progressed through elementary school. When I moved to the central office, I was concerned about losing that connection and seeing students grow over the years. What I didn't anticipate was developing connections with parents instead. Thanks to the ease of communication in our digital age, I periodically receive updates from parents about their children. I delight in seeing where their children are now in their lives, having persevered and grown. I am grateful to their parents for the trust they placed in me then, and I marvel that they take the time to continue to share their children with me now.

Reflection Question

How are you already addressing the whole child in your practice? What strategies from this chapter can you implement to enhance what you're already doing?

References

Betts, G. (2016, November 10). *The whole gifted child*. www.nagc.org/blog/whole-gifted-child

Boorman, H. (2018). *The gifted kids workbook: Mindfulness skills to help children reduce stress, balance emotions, and build confidence*. Instant Help Books.

Burnap, G. W. (1848). *Spheres and duties of woman: Course of lectures* (2nd ed.). John Murphy.

CAST. (2022). *About universal design for learning*. www.cast.org/impact/universal-design-for-learning-udl

The Whole Gifted Child Task Force. (2018). *Report to the NAGC board of directors*. National Association for Gifted Children. www.nagc.org/sites/default/files/key%20reports/4.1%20WGC%20Task%20Force%20Report.pdf

Resources

Galbraith, J. (2013). *The survival guide for gifted kids: For ages 10 and under*. Free Spirit.

Isaacson, K. L., & Fisher, T. J. (2007). *Intelligent life in the classroom: Smart kids and their teachers*. Great Potential Press.

Robinson, A., Adelson, J. L., Kidd, K., & Cunningham, C. M. (2018). A talent for tinkering: Developing talents in children from low-income households through engineering curriculum. *Gifted Child Quarterly*, *62*(1), 130–144. http://doi.org/10.1171/0016986217738049

6

The Importance of Educator Growth

Most teachers simply aren't prepared to teach students with gifts and talents (Crutchfield & Inman, 2020). In fact, "as of 2018, only five states required gifted coursework in preservice teacher and administrator training, while four states required inservice training" (p. 475). They are even less prepared for identifying and serving gifted learners from diverse backgrounds. After one or two courses on teaching learners from diverse backgrounds, educators reported that they still felt unprepared to teach this population (Nieto, 2013). Toss in gifts and talents, and the typical classroom teacher can be at a real loss. The same is true with teaching 2e learners, according to the National 2e Community of Practice: "Working successfully with this unique population [2e students] requires specialized academic training and ongoing professional development" (Association for the Education of Gifted Underachieving Students, n.d., para. 4). For the vast majority of teachers in the United States, that simply isn't happening. When professional learning does occur, it takes many forms: online coursework, book study, workshops, and mentoring are only a few. Just as student services differ to match readiness or interest, so should professional learning experiences differ so that educators may match their readiness levels in understanding and teaching gifted children to the learning opportunity.

DOI: 10.4324/9781003259190-6

Although this chapter won't serve as a one-hour graduate course in gifted education, it will provide sound advice for administrators and educators of children with gifts and talents. Anne N. Rinn, one of the authors of the *2018–2019 State of the States in Gifted Education* (2020), emphasized both the importance of understanding the concept of gifted education and the critical role that appropriate preparation makes for educators:

> Your definition of giftedness frames the ways in which you think about identifying students for gifted services, how you will serve students in gifted programs, if and how you will address gifted students' social and emotional experiences, whether giftedness is something that lasts beyond high school, and more. If you do not know your definition of giftedness, read *Paradigms of Gifted Education* (Dai & Chen, 2014), *Conceptions of Giftedness and Talent* (Sternberg & Ambrose, 2021), *Conceptual Frameworks for Giftedness and Talent Development* (Cross & Olszewski-Kubilius, 2020), and *From Giftedness to Gifted Education* (Plucker et al., 2017).
>
> In the *2018–2019 State of the States in Gifted Education* report (Rinn et al., 2020), results from a national survey show that the vast majority of states do not require training in gifted education for pre-service teacher candidates, administrators, or counselors. Training in gifted education for teachers of the gifted varies widely if it exists. Everyone on a campus is responsible for the education of all children, including children identified for gifted services. Everyone on a campus should therefore also have some training in gifted education.
>
> (personal communication, June 13, 2022)

What does that training look like? What should it comprise? Read suggestions and strategies from a variety of stakeholders to get some answers to those questions.

All Need Training

"You are describing my child."
"Why did I not know this sooner?"
"I didn't realize a student could be gifted if he had a learning disability!"
"Now I see why grades may not be a good criterion for determining giftedness."
These are common statements from teachers participating in professional learning in gifted education. The lives of gifted children are impacted in positive ways by the new knowledge and understandings of their teachers. School becomes a place of challenge and learning growth rather than a place of boredom and repetition. It is critical that all teachers be trained to recognize and meet the needs of advanced students.
  Mary Evans, former teacher in elementary, special education, and gifted education; former principal; program developer; and adjunct education professor

Find Mentors Then Pay It Forward

I cannot underestimate the power my mentors had on my chosen path of a 30-plus-year career advocating for gifted learners. I was fortunate to have mentors in the form of colleagues, school administrators, coordinators of gifted, and professors. All had vision and the knowhow to carry out this vision. Most importantly, they had the dedication and drive to make others around them better. Gather all the nuggets of wisdom you can from these gems, then pay it forward with promising educators in your life.
  Cheryl McCullough, former state president of gifted association and NAGC Board Member

Part of that professional learning should include details about the role you play as well as advice on how to play that role.

Everyone Has Something to Contribute

As a teacher, I do not enter the classroom as the expert. I recognize that those days of the faculty being the expert are over, particularly given the access our students have to information. Instead, I enter the classroom as a facilitator, conversation generator, and a catalyst for student learning. This does not mean that I do not bring expertise to the table; rather, it is the exact opposite. To teach gifted students today, you have to have a mastery of course content knowledge but also an ability to tap potential in students and assist them in developing as critical thinkers.

Stella L. Smith, associate director for a university center focusing on minorities, achievement, creativity, and high ability

Don't Be Intimidated

Working with gifted children can be intimidating at times, which is often one of the reasons I hear when people explain why they don't want to teach advanced classes. When working with gifted children, especially those who are really advanced, I like to set the tone by letting everyone know that none of us in the class knows everything and that we are going to learn together this year. When I start my classes with this mindset, it allows students to be more open with new and challenging material.

Justin Mitchell, eighth-grade social studies teacher and school gifted coordinator

A Bad Day

I often tell my undergraduate teacher candidates, "If you walk out of your classroom at the end of the day, and you haven't learned something new from your students – you have probably had a bad day." For me, one of the greatest joys of teaching is learning as much from my students as I hope they learn from me. Our students come to us with rich experiences and traditions. When we open our hearts to their stories – who they are beyond the classroom – we create an environment where cultures and traditions are honored, respected, and engrained in all that we do.

C. Matthew Fugate, one of Variation's *magazine's 22 People to Watch in the neurodiversity movement*

Once you realize that your students are your partners in both teaching and learning, and once your students realize that you respect them as people and scholars, you will be able to connect with them in ways you never imagined. Your authentic relationships contribute to a learning community that is safe for taking risks, rich with challenge, and respectful of all.

The Authentic Educator

I have observed that the most successful teachers and administrators are those who are authentic, have a genuine love and interest in their students, and who use relational pedagogy. That is, they promote instructional processes, strategies, and activities designed to not only increase academic achievement and mastery of learning, but also to have a connection that empowers and encourages students to include any element of their culture, ethnicity, or language in demonstrating what they know and are able to do. Even at very young ages, gifted students know the difference between an educator who is authentic and one who is simply going through the motions. Acknowledging victories and struggles is part of relationship building. The authentic educator asks the students questions when unsure, victories are celebrated together, and struggles become problem-solving opportunities.

Jaime Castellano, preeminent scholar and researcher in gifted education and in identifying and serving diverse/special populations of gifted students

Healthy learning communities include hard work and laughter.

Make Room for Dessert

Most of us consider dessert to be the best part of the meal, yet, in my years waiting tables, rarely did customers ever order it. Your job will be hard, daunting at times. You will spend hours working on strategies, years tweaking and improving them. Be careful not to fill up on the preparation and implementation, working so tirelessly to make a difference that you don't take time to reflect and enjoy the changes you see.

They will be subtle, and it may take years to see the impact fully realized; nevertheless, when you see them, rejoice! It's okay to take pride in your work.

Vicki Cooper, gifted endorsed teacher and specialist in district level administration

Humor

Humor is a powerful tool. Laughter allows us to release stress and to express joy in the short term. Over the long term, laughter can improve mood, boost your immune system, and may even help relieve pain. Unfortunately, I see it too often used to demean or poke at others. When used well, humor can connect us through shared experiences and help us put things in their proper perspective. Laughing at yourself, your challenges, and your mistakes will model healthy coping skills for those gifted and 2e kids around us who may be struggling. It may even help fend off unhealthy perfectionism in yourself. Find ways to use humor to build up, recharge, or simply have fun! Ridicule and humiliation, even when done with attempted humor, do not inspire, encourage, or motivate. Use your sense of humor for good, not evil!

Edward R. Amend, co-author of the award-winning Misdiagnosis and Dual Diagnoses of Gifted Children and Adults: ADHD, Bipolar, OCD, Asperger's, Depression, and Other Disorders (2nd ed.)

Strategically using our healthy sense of humor, realizing it's perfectly okay to not be the smartest person in the room, understanding the nuances of gifted learners both as people and students, and all the other ideas mentioned here require two foundational concepts: reflection and self-care.

Reflect on Your Practice

One of the things that has made me a better teacher is to constantly reflect on my practice. To help me become better, I keep a journal of reflections throughout the year. On a regular basis, I will add notes

about lessons, changes I need to make for the next year, student misconceptions on topics, and just a place for ideas. This reflection is kept electronically, which allows me to share with my content partner, so we can better put these things into practice. At the end of the year, I also enjoy discussing with students what they thought was good and what needs to be changed for the next group of students.
Justin Mitchell, secretary of state gifted association
and chair of state Education Professional
Standards Board

Self-Care

Stressed-out? Anxious? You should do self-care, but what is that really? Martin Seligman, the "Father of Positive Psychology," proposes a helpful model of happiness with three things you can do. The Pleasant Life comprises sensory things that make you feel better: bubble bath, shopping, comedy. Mindfulness. These work, but you need them frequently. The Good Life means that you connect with friends and family. You need your support network. The third, and the most long-lasting, is focusing on the Meaningful Life – helping others and doing work that matters. The best self-care is caring for others. Combine them all and build a house for Habitat for Humanity with friends!
Claire Hughes, professor of twice-exceptional and gifted
programs and mother of two 2e young people

Our growth as teachers ultimately depends on us. Just as our students hold responsibility for their learning, we hold responsibility for ours. In a perfect world, every preservice teacher would learn about the nature and needs of students with gifts and talents, including best practices in identification and services through the lens of equity, access, and opportunity for all. Some of their clinical experience would take place in gifted classrooms. Practicing teachers would continue that learning (do I dare include via fully funded federal and state mandates?) through ongoing, embedded, and differentiated professional learning experiences. And we would be called to work in a way that is greater than the self. Let equity-minded administrator, educational consultant, and author April Wells explain:

> Our ability to lift the timely and timeless work in the field includes a willingness for us to suspend our disbelief. Exchanging judgement for curiosity or wonderment permits us to gain insight into the field. This shapes how we engage and ultimately positions us to participate as brokers partnering with students, families, and stakeholders to leave gifted and talented education better than we found it. All that we do adds to a collective lift that makes a difference for students who desperately need us. We're called to this work in a way that is greater than the self. May we represent well.

> **Sharing Joy: Thanks for Understanding**
>
> Marissa Wilkerson, interventionist endorsed in gifted education
>
> In my last year of teaching fifth grade, I encountered a child who was exceptionally gifted, identified in General Intellect and Specific Academic Aptitude in Language Arts and Math. Along with her high academic ability came intense pressure from not only the adults around her at school and at home but also from herself. This child was motivated to grow, but she was unsure of how successful she could be. She would get discouraged if she did not score perfectly and needed guidance along the way. This student had to overcome several obstacles, and she persevered through hard work and determination. Over the course of the year, I offered her guidance, words of encouragement, and strategies to help her reach her potential. At the end of year, this child wrote me a letter saying, "Thank you for understanding me." At that moment, I knew that I could truly make a difference with every child.

Sharing Joy: The Real Deal

Cheryl McCullough, gifted services supervisor who has worked in gifted education for 30 years

As a new supervisor in a new school system, I had much to prove to my colleagues. I took a risk and asked a principal if I could take over three summer school classes. Hiring three phenomenal resource teachers for the gifted, they implemented gifted curriculum with scaffolding instead of using remediation strategies being used in other classes. After our last day, the supervisor of Equity and Excellence stopped me in the parking lot saying she was blown away by the culturally responsive pedagogy she saw in those classrooms and said we were the "real deal."

Sharing Joy: Professional Recognition

Fred A. Bonner II, professor, endowed chair, and director of a university center for minority, achievement, creativity, and high ability

I was filled with joy when Donald Ambrose contacted me to ask if I would participate in an interview with *Roeper Review* to discuss my experiences as a scholar in the field of gifted education. When Don mentioned how this interview would situate me among some of the legendary scholars in the field – all scholars whom I greatly respected like Donna Ford, Joseph Renzulli, and Robert Sternberg – it brought me extreme joy to know that my research and scholarship were seen as contributing to the field. This joyous moment was only paralleled by the actual publication of the interview.

> **Sharing Joy: Seize the Opportunity**
>
> Kurshanna J. Dean, presidential appointee on NAGC Board of Directors with more than 20 years of experience in gifted education
>
> Walking into a room filled with gifted experts can be overwhelming – at least it was for me, an instructional specialist standing in for the director of Accelerated and Enriched Instruction. I served on a panel alongside leading gifted experts during the 2014 NAGC Convention. Sitting on that panel was the most intimidating, invigorating experience of my career. I seized the opportunity to raise my voice in an effort to call for an increase in gifted programming for students regardless of their racial and socioeconomic status. This was the beginning – 6 years later I was invited to join NAGC's board of directors.

Reflection Question

What sort of training in gifted education are you most interested in or curious about? How can you incorporate these topics into an ongoing, differentiated professional learning plan?

References

Association for the Education of Gifted Underachieving Students. (n.d.). *Our work*. www.aegus1.com/our-work

Cross, T. L., & Olszewski-Kubilius, P. (Eds.). (2020). *Conceptual frameworks for giftedness and talent development: Enduring theories and comprehensive models in gifted education*. Routledge.

Crutchfield, K., & Inman, T. F. (2020). Teacher preparation and gifted education. In J. A. Plucker & C. M. Callahan (Eds.), *Critical issues and practices in gifted education: A survey of current research on giftedness and talent development* (3rd ed., pp. 471–484). Prufrock Academic Press.

Dai, D. Y., & Chen, F. (2014). *Paradigms of gifted education: A guide to theory-based, practice-focused research*. Prufrock Press.

Nieto, S. (2013). *Finding joy in teaching students of diverse backgrounds: Culturally responsive and socially just practices in U.S. classrooms*. Heinemann.

Plucker, J. A., Rinn, A. N., & Makel, M. C. (Eds.). (2017). *From giftedness to gifted education: Reflecting theory in practice*. Prufrock Press.

Rinn, A. N., Mun, R. U., & Hodges, J. (2020). *2018–2019 state of the states in gifted education*. National Association for Gifted Children and the Council of State Directors of Programs for the Gifted.

Sternberg, R. J., & Ambrose, D. (Eds.). (2021). *Conceptions of giftedness and talent*. Palgrave Macmillan.

7

The Advocate

Most of us readily understand the importance of advocating for veteran health care, refugee relocation, and social security. We encourage our leaders to put tax dollars to use for research and solutions. Some of us transfer advocacy to education, especially in terms of at-risk students or students with disabilities. Advocacy in the 1970s ultimately led to the current Individuals with Disabilities Education Act (IDEA; P. L. 108–446) which revolutionized learning for children who had one or more disabilities; these included everything from deaf-blindness to intellectual disability, from speech impairment to autism. Billions of federal dollars, such as the $16 billion in 2022, continue to support IDEA (Office of Management and Budget, 2022). Its impact on our nation and people is immeasurable, and it wouldn't have happened when it did if not for advocates helping Congress and the nation understand its importance. We readily comprehend the need to help children with traumatic brain injuries, specific learning disabilities, or emotional disturbances. Too few of us, however, link exceptionality to learners with gifts and talents. They simply don't look needy. For example, reading three grades above level pales in comparison to a fourth grader not reading at all, yet these are both needs. For the gifted, needs come from strengths, not deficiencies.

DOI: 10.4324/9781003259190-7

Every single child, regardless of label, has the right to learn something new every day. However, the decades-long emphasis on proficiency helped stagnate progress of our high-ability students. Federal and state budgets allocate monies to what is considered important by the leadership. Federally, the government allotted $13 million to gifted education in 2022. This funding must be used for federal research. The fiduciary onus falls on state governments – that may or may not include gifted education in their budgets. Amounts ranged from $0 to $76,623,596.20 in 2020–2021 (Rinn et al., 2022), but most states dictate how that money is spent. In my home state, Kentucky, 75% must be spent on personnel (Programs for the gifted and talented, 1990). Check out your state at this website: www.nagc.org/gifted-state.

Of course, increasing funding is only one advocacy point. Laws, policies, and procedures can remove learning ceilings for students – or strengthen the already-low ceilings. It's our job as educators, citizens, and advocates for children to learn about laws, policies, and procedures, and then look at them through the lens of high-ability learners. You will find many have unintentional consequences that could prove limiting to a child with gifts and talents. For example, a school policy that offers College Board Advanced Placement classes only for their juniors and seniors may cause freshmen and sophomores to place learning on hold for a couple of years. Jonathan Plucker, who coined the term *Excellence Gap*, encourages us to ask policy makers and educators two questions before any policy is passed:

- ◆ How will this policy impact advanced students?
- ◆ How will this policy help more students perform at advanced levels?

(n.d., p. 1, par. 9)

The following ideas include tips and strategies from people who have asked these two questions. From self-advocacy to national advocacy, it's vital that we take a stand. Perhaps these responses can encourage you to advocate.

A district offering to pay for a gifted endorsement encouraged this parent and educator to learn how to advocate for her daughter and others like her.

A Catalyst for Change

When presented the opportunity to become GT certified by my district, I was quick to accept. At that time my oldest daughter was one of my motivating factors. Too often minority students are overlooked in the areas of general intelligence and only noticed for their performance talents such as athletic prowess or performing arts. Black girls, such as my daughters, are particularly disregarded for intellectual giftedness in the areas of STEM and leadership capabilities. Thanks to my certification, I am now able to advocate on behalf of all students and be a voice for those who are often overlooked by helping to educate others about characteristics of gifted children and performance indicators to look for. It is my hope that I can continue to shed light on this disparity even from outside of the classroom and to somehow be a catalyst for meaningful change.

Patrice Johnson, fourth-grade regular classroom teacher and mother of two gifted children

Sharing information is a vital way to advocate for gifted learners.

Collaboration Is Key

Gifted education can be isolating if you let it be. Many gifted learners spend most of their day in general education classroom settings with teachers and/or administrators who may or may not understand the needs of diverse gifted learners. The same may be true for educators working in gifted education. With the varying needs in classrooms today, gifted services may not be seen as a priority for many decision makers. Relationship building and collaboration are essential at all stages of a school systems hierarchy if the needs of gifted learners are to be addressed in a comprehensive way.

Cheryl McCullough, NBCT supervisor of gifted education and recipient of Mover and Shaker of Virginia's Future Problem Solvers

Be(A)Ware of Myths

One of the biggest challenges facing gifted education is wading through the misconceptions regarding the field. Educate everyone surrounding gifted learners. Have weekly tips, monthly newsletters, or negotiate 5 to 10 minutes at monthly faculty meetings. Whatever method you choose, make your knowledge available and heard. In my 13th year in this position, I am still combating myths. To be truly effective, the majority of gifted instruction and rigor must come from inside the classroom. It is difficult to implement effective instruction if instructors are off base from reality. The only way to ever defeat these myths and erase them from practice is to consistently communicate the message.

Vicki Cooper, district gifted education coordinator for a rural school district

Be Careful What You Say

Teachers should be cautious about engaging in negative speech concerning any group of students, including gifted students. Some teachers subscribe to the paradigm that gifted students feel they are better than their nongifted peers due to their high abilities. This negative misperception is detrimental to gifted students who experience challenges and troubles just like their nongifted peers do. Some teachers believe gifted classes are perfect wonderlands of instruction, but that could not be further from the truth.

Justin Moreschi, fourth-grade science teacher with a specialist in gifted education

Listen

Listen. Each stakeholder has a different perspective and belief on gifted education and where we should be traveling on this educational journey. As a leader, listening to district leaders, principals, teachers, families, community partners, and students has encouraged me to be an intentional thought partner. The dialogues have allowed me to plan opportunities for a more inclusive gifted education program. Listening has allowed me to be more open minded in leading our district to a more inclusive gifted programming and dismantling the elitism we face in gifted education.

Julie Gann, district gifted coordinator and a change agent for gifted and talented students

It is just as important to advocate for individuals and teach students how to advocate for themselves as it is to build advocacy in others by teaching them about gifted education.

A Tip for 2e

As a staff developer and gifted specialist, I often find myself working to convince teachers that gifted students have needs just like students who qualify for Individual Education Plans (IEPs) for their exceptionalities. One strategy I have learned is to use the word **neurodiverse** *in conjunction with or in place of the word* **gifted**. *This helps teachers and administrators see that the brains of our GT students are actually different in the way that they process the world, and that they have their own unique socioemotional and intellectual needs that need to be met to ensure their success in classrooms and beyond.*

Sarah Yost, NBCT educator in public schools for almost 25 years

A Teacher's Power

I loved school as a child. Each day was an exciting blend of new information, class discussion, and time with friends. At night around the dinner table, my sisters and I shared our experiences with caring parents who delighted in our achievements and supported our endeavors. I was lucky. Some of my classmates returned home to empty houses, ate dinner in silence, and went to bed without the benefit of a caring adult. As educators, we have opportunities to provide so much more than a standards-based curriculum. A caring adult can affirm student ability and advocate on their behalf. We have the power to help students believe in themselves and their future. When we do, they do.

Wendy A. Behrens, national and international presenter on the identification of underserved populations, comprehensive service design, and policies that support highly able learners

Preparing Advocates

In my school, gifted services are all about equity and social justice because our students come from groups that have historically been underrepresented in gifted classes. Helping to identify and serve our high-poverty Black and Brown gifted students' needs means empowering them to know their own strengths and capabilities, even if they aren't receiving affirming messages elsewhere. Part of my work is not just advocating for our gifted students to be challenged intellectually, but also preparing them to advocate for their own right to be educated at their appropriate level in middle and high school.

Sarah Yost, NBCT President for her state from 2020–2022

Show What You Know

Don't be afraid to be an advocate. Gifted students find me. Even at the university level where students are not identified, the gifted students find me. They know through my passions and interests that gifted education is important at all stages of learning. I support students to find what they need in terms of graduate programs, career planning, and life situations. They know I will work with them to find what they need. I am not necessarily their advisor, but the students gravitate to me. It's a role that is not in my job description that I cherish.

Megan Parker Peters, internationally known psychologist who works primarily with gifted and 2e learners

Parents, caregivers, and families must be included in advocacy efforts as well. Their voices are often heard more clearly than others' voices. We must help them learn all they can about their children.

Meeting to Set Gifted Goals With Parents

A powerful synergy happens when gifted teachers meet in person with parents or the adults in the child's life and the gifted child to set goals. Mutual understanding and support can come as relationships are built on trust and common interest in seeing the child succeed. These meetings can happen in traditional ways such as during parent-teacher conference time. They can also come in the form of a home visit, an IEP meeting, or even a casual meet-up for coffee before school. To get the most out of these meetings, teachers need to be ready to listen twice as much as they speak. When setting goals together, the child's strengths, interests, and future goals will remain at the center of the conversation when they attend the meeting too.

> Jessica LaFollette, president of her state association and incoming chair for NAGC's Parent, Family, and Community Network

Parents Need Support, Too

In gifted education, we focus the majority of our attention on what students need, particularly in schools every day. When we discuss parents and families, it is through the lens of educating them about what their children need. However, parents need support, too. They need the opportunity to be heard and to connect with others who are parenting gifted and talented children. They need to be able to talk about their experiences and to share their fears and hopes with others. Just as our gifted and talented students need a community of peers, their parents need a community. By helping parents connect with one another, educators impact students beyond the school building.

> Lynette Breedlove, treasurer of her state advocacy organization and former president of The Association for the Gifted

My mom taught me to always pass on a compliment when I heard one. Perhaps Jonathan's mom, in the next piece, did as well. Relaying compliments may be viewed as a unique form of advocacy, but empowering educators and others who care about gifted education and talent development with confidence helps them continue their work.

Appreciation

Few things mean more to a teacher than hearing from a student years after you've taught them. But in my experience, former students are more likely to tell others about influential teachers rather than the teachers themselves. I often meet people who have connections to someone I know or somewhere I've worked. They share variations of "so-and-so was tough, but I often think about the things she taught me." Be the person who contacts that teacher or professor to share the positive feedback. In this age when criticism can be shared instantly with thousands of people, making a little extra effort to share former students' positive comments with their teachers and professors is one way to push back against the waves of negativity we all face as teachers!
Jonathan Plucker, an educational psychologist and endowed professor of talent development who examines education policy and talent development

Advocacy ranges from serving on a national board for gifted children to talking to your child's teacher about challenges, to everything in between. Know that you are the voice for those who will be powerful voices in the future. We must teach others how to advocate.

Sharing of Joy: Creating Change

Dina Brulles, gifted program coordinator at a state university and former gifted education director

We hold incredible power for creating change in our systems.
I recently retired from K–12 education after having served as a gifted coordinator for more than two decades. I feel incredibly fortunate for having been able to influence my school districts' teachers and school administrators in recognizing, understanding, and supporting our gifted

learners. Most of us do this privately, in our own silos. Though collectively, we are committed and passionate educators, and we hold incredible power for creating change in our systems. I have learned that even incremental changes can profoundly impact the lives of the gifted learners we strive to nurture. And incremental changes lead to lasting and sustainable outcomes upon which others can build. Collaborate with others sharing these goals; our voices are stronger together.

Sharing of Joy: The Value of Hard Work

Julie Gann, 2021 recipient of NAGC's Gifted Coordinator Award

The saying "hard work really does pay off" rings true in my current work. Over the past several years, I have worked tirelessly with my team to instill advocacy within our district – advocacy that would ensure opportunity and access for each of our students. We have instilled this by building relationships with our faculty, district leaders, and community partners. We have provided consistent procedures and communication to our stakeholders. Training school-level and district support staff on gifted education and allowing for stakeholders to be part of this process has instituted an inclusive gifted educational system in our district. Creating partnerships and building relationships at each level of the educational world, I am now beginning to see the fruit of our labor. Classroom teachers are advocating, principals are advocating, and district-level personnel are advocating for our gifted students to get the programming services they need daily. We still have a way to go, but to see the dismantling of the elitist stigma (albeit slowly) has been a great feeling!

Sharing of Joy: Gifted and Gay

Paul James "PJ" Sedillo, author of award-winning book *Solidarity Through Pride* and associate professor in a special and gifted education department

Throughout my life, I had to decide when and when not to "come out" as a gay gifted male. I feared losing my job or being beaten up (common in my city as well as across the US). I remember attending a gay pride parade in my hometown, watching from the sidelines. When the camera crew arrived, I hid, so they wouldn't film me. When I went home, I cried. I realized my life needed to change from walking around with my head hanging low, heartbroken with an aching soul, knees shaking that people would find out, and ready to quit living. That is when I realized I was tired of not being true to myself.

My misery changed to an internal anger, which eventually became a self-actualization: I was a proud gay man. Loved by God, I was an awesome human being. I didn't deserve to hide in the shadows for fear of revealing my true self. This rebirth moved me into a new light, gave me a new identity and hope. Pure joy came about with this transformation.

I soon became the voice for others in my community, state, and nation, encouraging them to obtain that same joy by honoring their true selves. Using my internal joy for strength, I advocated for (and won) job protection for LGBTQ teachers within the Albuquerque Public School System, then moved on to obtain full spousal health benefits from the school district. I eventually would fight for the rights of gifted LGBTQ individuals by opening the eyes of others.

Reflection Question

How do you advocate for the students in your school, district, or state? What can you do to teach students how to advocate for themselves?

References

Individuals with Disabilities Education Improvement Act of 2004, Public Law 446, U.S. Statutes at Large 118 (2004): 2647–2808. https://www.govinfo.gov/app/details/PLAW-108publ446

Office of Management and Budget. (2022). *Budget of the U.S. government: Fiscal year 2022*. www.whitehouse.gov/wp-content/uploads/2021/05/budget_fy22.pdf

Plucker, J. A. (n.d.). *Excellence gaps in Kentucky*. www.wku.edu/gifted/documents/excellence-gaps-brochure.pdf

Programs for the Gifted and Talented. (1990). *704 KAR 3:285*. https://apps.legislature.ky.gov/law/kar/titles/704/003/285/

Rinn, A. N., Mun, R. U., & Hodges, J. (2022). *2020–2021 State of the states in gifted education*. National Association for Gifted Children and the Council of State Directors of Programs for the Gifted.

8

Looking Through the Lens of Potential

So, how many notes do you have scrawled in the margins? Are pages dog-eared? How many tried-and-true ideas have you shared with a colleague? More importantly, have you reflected on the joys "this work" has brought you? Perhaps you have colorful Post-it notes stuck to your bathroom mirror, glove box, monitor, or filing cabinet, each detailing a child, a recognition, an aha, an idea, a hug. Perhaps they have single names on them: Mateo, Abdul, Molly, Kai, Lucas. I'm sure just hearing the name "Molly" brings a soft smile to the face of Thomas P. Hébert just as "Seth" or "LJ" lights up Debbie Dailey's face. Maybe you have a phrase taken from one of the strategies or stories: Sandra N. Kaplan's *Spill-Over Effect*, Vicki Cooper's *Be(A)Ware of Myths*, Todd Stanley's *You Can Teach an Old Dog New Tricks*, Jaime Castellano's *Bill of Rights*, or Tamara Fisher Alley's *Cutting Them Loose*. Perhaps you have a time you ran into a grateful former student as Joy Lawson Davis (their self-proclaimed at-risk student who became part of a Fortune 500 company) and Wendy A. Behrens ("See that lady? She told Daddy he was good at math.") did.

I hope that you thought of your own practices, ideas, and stories of joy that you can share with others. I also hope you made a list of concepts and strategies that you are eager to learn about in greater depth. Perhaps the term *neurodiversity* is new to you, or you want to explore how to set up a mentorship for teachers or address the whole child.

Above all, I hope you rediscovered or enhanced your commitment to and love of these extraordinary people – which brings you joy.

Just as April Wells submitted the perfect opening for the book with her poem *This Work*, award-winning author Mary Cay Ricci turned in an ideal ending. Disregarding the instructions of submitting a critical insight, this creative thinker, this gifted kid grown-up, decided to issue a challenge instead. (Personally, I am thrilled she didn't let parameters constrict her thinking or thwart her creativity.) So I will leave you with her submission, and I hope you'll share with me what you find.

Believe in the Children

Rather than a critical insight, I would like to initiate a challenge to every educator reading this. I challenge you to look at every child through a lens of potential. Find the potential that a child holds within them instead of focusing on those things that may get in the way. Things that can negatively influence our thinking about a child's achievement include language, behaviors, socioeconomic status, race, and special needs. Remember that test scores and grades represent a moment in time, not what the future could be for a child. So many children are underchallenged, and we must commit to nurturing the potential in everyone. Let's consider all of the possibilities in the wonderful children that surround us!

Reflection Question

What memories come to mind when you contemplate moments of joy in your own practice? What kinds of joy do you look forward to experiencing in the future?

Biographies of Contributors

Tamara Fisher Alley, M.A., is the K–12 Gifted Education Specialist for Polson Schools on Montana's Flathead Indian Reservation. She is past president of Montana AGATE and writes "Unwrapping the Gifted" for NAGC's *Teaching for High Potential*. Tamara was selected 2001 Polson Teacher of the Year and 2013 Montana AGATE Educator of the Year.

Edward R. Amend, Psy.D., a clinical psychologist at The Amend Group in Lexington, KY, focuses on the social, emotional, and educational needs of gifted, twice-exceptional, and neurodiverse youth, adults, and their families. His service has included various leadership roles with the National Association for Gifted Children (NAGC), Supporting Emotional Needs of the Gifted (SENG), and *The G WORD* film's Advisory Board.

Wendy A. Behrens, M.A.E., is the Gifted Education Specialist for the Minnesota Department of Education, advising educators, families, and policymakers. She frequently presents to national and international audiences on the identification of underserved populations, comprehensive service design, and policies that support highly able learners. Wendy is president-elect of The Association for the Gifted (TAG), a division of the Council for Exceptional Children.

Fred A. Bonner II, Ed.D., is Professor, Endowed Chair, and Minority, Achievement, Creativity, High-Ability (MACH-III) Center Director at Prairie View A&M University. Fred's scholarship has a multidisciplinary focus on diversity, equity, inclusion, and belonging, with a particular emphasis on the experiences of academically gifted African American males across the P–20 education pipeline.

Lynette Breedlove, Ph.D., serves as the director of the residential program Carol M. Gatton Academy of Mathematics and

Science in Kentucky. She has held multiple leadership roles on several boards of gifted education advocacy organizations including the state associations in Kentucky and Texas, TAG, and NAGC.

Dina Brulles, Ph.D., is the former Gifted Education Director at Paradise Valley USD and the Gifted Program Coordinator at Arizona State University. She serves as Governance Secretary for NAGC. Dina's work and publications center on increasing inclusion and building equity in gifted education programs and services using culturally responsive practices.

Jaime Castellano, Ph.D., is a nationally recognized and award-winning educator, principal, author, scholar, and researcher. In 2017 he was recognized as SENG's National Educator of the Year. He is a preeminent scholar and researcher in gifted education and in identifying and serving diverse/special populations of gifted students.

Vicki Cooper, Ed.S., holds a master's degree in secondary education, an education specialist degree in district-level administration and an endorsement in gifted education. She has spent 13 years as the district gifted education coordinator for a rural school district.

Tracy L. Cross, Ph.D., holds an endowed chair, Jody and Layton Smith Professor of Psychology and Gifted Education, and is the executive director of both the Center for Gifted Education and the Institute for Research on the Suicide of Gifted Students at William & Mary. He has published more than 200 articles, book chapters, and columns; made more than 300 presentations at conferences; and published 14 books.

Debbie Dailey, Ed.D., is an associate professor of education and chair in the Department of Teaching and Learning at the University of Central Arkansas. She also serves as president of TAG. Prior to moving to higher education, Debbie was a high school science and gifted education teacher for 20 years.

Joy Lawson Davis, Ed.D., is an award-winning educator who has devoted her work to increasing equity in gifted education.

She has served in many leadership roles, holds two degrees in gifted education, and is also a keynote speaker and international consultant. She is author of many publications, including the recent book *Empowering Underrepresented Gifted Students*.

Kurshanna J. Dean, M.A., with 20 years of experience in gifted education, was named 2020 Outstanding Educator in a Local School System – Gifted and Talented Coordinator by the Maryland State Department of Education. Kurshanna is a presidential appointee on NAGC Board of Directors as well as former supervisor of Accelerated and Enriched Instruction in Montgomery County Public Schools.

Jim Delisle, Ph.D., has worked with and for gifted students for more than 40 years, as a teacher, counselor, and professor. The author of 26 books, including the best-selling *Gifted Teen Survival Guide* (with Judy Galbraith), Jim continues to consult worldwide on issues related to gifted students' social and emotional growth.

Brittany M. Dodds, Psy.D., NCSP, is a public-school psychologist and adjunct instructor. Brittany has worked in the field of school psychology since 2014, serving in districts across south-central Kentucky and northern Virginia. She has presented on the state, national, and international levels.

Mary Evans, Ed.D., has taught regular elementary, special education, and gifted education in public schools in Missouri and served as an elementary principal in Kentucky. She is a program developer for The Center for Gifted Studies at Western Kentucky University where she teaches graduate classes and provides professional development in gifted education.

C. Matthew Fugate, Ph.D., has researched and presented on topics including the social-emotional needs of twice-exceptional students, culturally responsive teaching, and creativity. He is active in NAGC and the Texas Association for Gifted and Talented. Matthew was recently named one of *Variations* magazine's 22 People to Watch in the neurodiversity movement.

Julie Gann, Ed.S., is the Gifted and Talented Coordinator for Fayette County Public Schools in Lexington, KY. In 2021, Julie was awarded NAGC's Gifted Coordinator Award. Julie has been a change agent for gifted and talented students in Fayette County, ensuring that students in her district have opportunity and access to gifted and talented programming and services.

Jessa Luckey Goudelock, Ph.D., is a gifted program director in Wichita, KS. She is a graduate of Howard University and the University of Georgia and was a 2019 NAGC Carolyn Callahan Doctoral Student Award winner. Jessa currently serves as the Parent Editorial Content & Advisory Board (PECAB) Chair for NAGC and Parent Committee member for Kansas Association for the Gifted, Talented, and Creative.

Thomas P. Hébert, Ph.D., is professor of gifted education at the University of South Carolina. Dr. Hébert has more than a decade of K–12 classroom experience working with gifted students and 25 years in higher education training graduate students and educators in gifted education.

Claire Hughes, Ph.D., is a professor of Twice Exceptional and Gifted Programs at Cleveland State University with a doctorate in both gifted education and special education from William & Mary. Her passion is helping teachers and parents find talents in all kids – especially kids with diverse backgrounds and/or disabilities.

Patrice Johnson, M.A., is a fourth-grade teacher with a gifted and talented endorsement at Jefferson County Public Schools. She has two daughters, Paige and Peyton, whom she credits as motivating factors for her to become GT certified.

Sandra N. Kaplan, Ed.D., a professor of Clinical Education in Rossier School of Education at University of Southern California, has focused on curriculum and instruction related to general and gifted education. She has written articles as well as designed and published curriculum in these areas and has worked as a consultant for districts within and outside of the United States.

Jessica LaFollette, Ph.D., has been teaching gifted students for over 20 years in Kansas City, KS. She is the president of the Kansas Association for the Gifted, Talented, and Creative as well as chair-elect of NAGC's Parent, Family, and Community Network. She is a graduate of Emporia State University and The University of Missouri-Kansas City.

Cheryl McCullough, Ed.S., supervises Gifted Services in Arlington, VA. Working in gifted education for 30 years, she has served on the NAGC Board and was president of Virginia Association for the Gifted. She earned National Board Certification, is an Adaptive School agency trainer, and was awarded the Mover and Shaker of Virginia's Future Problem Solvers.

Justin Mitchell, M.A., is an eighth-grade social studies teacher and Gifted & Talented Coordinator at Franklin-Simpson Middle School in Kentucky. He was named the 2021 Kentucky History Teacher of the Year and was the National History Teacher of the Year Finalist. Justin serves as Secretary of the Kentucky Association for Gifted Education.

Felicia M. G. Moreschi, Ed.S., began her teaching career in 2013. She teaches fifth-grade social studies and has worked extensively with gifted students in an urban school setting. She completed a specialist degree in Gifted Education and Talent Development in 2022.

Justin Moreschi, Ed.S., is a fourth-grade science teacher from Louisville, KY, where he has been teaching since 2007. He is certified in primary through fifth-grade elementary education, primary through 12th special education, and gifted education. Justin completed his specialist degree in gifted education in 2022.

Angela Novak, Ph.D., is an assistant professor at East Carolina University. Angela has served NAGC and TAG in a variety of roles, including Board, Committee, and Network leadership positions. She has published articles and book chapters, and presented at state, national, and international conferences on equity in gifted education.

Megan Parker Peters, Ph.D., is an associate professor at Lipscomb University. Megan has served NAGC and the Tennessee Association for the Gifted in a variety of leadership roles. A psychologist who works primarily with gifted and 2e learners, Megan has published articles and book chapters, and presented at state, national, and international conferences on psychosocial needs of gifted learners.

Jonathan Plucker, Ph.D., is the Julian C. Stanley Professor of Talent Development at Johns Hopkins University, where he works at the Center for Talented Youth and School of Education. A former elementary school science teacher, he now studies creativity, talent development, and equity in advanced education. He is a prolific author and presenter.

Michael Postma, Ed.D., is a teacher, administrator, consultant, speaker, and author dedicated to the holistic development of both gifted and twice-exceptional children through his company Gifted & Thriving, LLC. Director of Programming for SENG, he is the father of four children, three of whom are twice-exceptional.

Joe Renzulli, Ed.D., is a leader and pioneer in gifted education and applying the pedagogy of gifted education teaching strategies to all students. The American Psychological Association named him among the 25 most influential psychologists in the world. He received the Harold W. McGraw, Jr. Award for Innovation in Education, considered by many to be "the Nobel" for educators and was a consultant to the White House Task Force on Education of the Gifted and Talented.

Mary Cay Ricci, M.A., wrote books on growth mindset for educators, parents, and kids as well as co-authored *Increasing Diversity in Gifted Education*. Now a national speaker and consultant, her experience includes elementary and middle school teacher, central office administrator, and instructional specialist.

Sylvia Rimm, Ph.D., a psychologist who directs Family Achievement Clinic in Ohio, specializes in gifted children. Her many books include *Education of the Gifted and Talented, Why Bright*

Kids Get Poor Grades, and best seller *See Jane Win®*. Once a regular contributor to NBC's *Today Show*, Sylvia also hosted public radio's *Family Talk*. She has received many awards for her contributions to gifted education.

Anne N. Rinn, Ph.D., is professor of Educational Psychology at the University of North Texas, as well as Director of the Office for Giftedness, Talent Development, and Creativity. She is the author of *Social, Emotional, and Psychosocial Development of Gifted and Talented Individuals* (2020) and was co-editor of the *Journal of Advanced Academics*.

Ann Robinson, Ph.D., is Distinguished Professor and Founding Director of the Jodie Mahony Center for Gifted Education, University of Arkansas-Little Rock. She is former editor of *Gifted Child Quarterly*; NAGC past-president; charter board member of the AERA Special Interest Group Research on Giftedness, Creativity and Talent Development; and associate editor for *Gifted and Talented International*.

Paul James "PJ" Sedillo, Ph.D., associate professor for the Special/Gifted Education Department at New Mexico Highlands University, has published many articles and chapters as well as *Solidarity Through Pride*, which won best book in Arizona/New Mexico for 2018. Former President for the NM Association for the Gifted, PJ has also served in multiple NAGC roles.

Stella L. Smith, Ph.D., serves as an assistant professor in the Department of Educational Leadership and Counseling and the associate director for the Minority Achievement, Creativity and High-Ability (MACH-III) Center at Prairie View A&M University.

Todd Stanley, M.A., is the author of many teacher-education books including *Project-Based Learning for Gifted Students (2nd ed.)*, *Promoting Rigor Through Higher-Level Questioning*, and *How the Hell Do We Motivate These Kids?* He served as classroom teacher for 18 years and is the gifted coordinator for Pickerington Schools. He also created a website rich with resources: www.thegiftedguy.com.

April Wells, M.A., is an equity-minded administrator, educational consultant, and author. She serves on the Board of Directors for the National Association for Gifted Children. Her work has served as inspiration for other organizations endeavoring to move the equity imperative in the field. April leads with compassion and urgency.

Marissa Wilkerson, M.S.Ed., an elementary teacher with a strong work ethic, has excellent rapport with students, colleagues, and parents and has a proactive, professional approach to education, especially with gifted learners. During her 15 years of teaching, she has supported all children both academically and emotionally. She now serves as a gifted and talented interventionist at an elementary school.

Sarah Yost, Ed.S., is a National Board-certified teacher (NBCT) and staff developer at Byck Elementary in Louisville, KY. She has worked in public education since 2005, and she served as the Kentucky NBCT President from 2020–2022. Sarah received her Gifted and Talented Education Specialist Endorsement at Western Kentucky University in 2021.

Taylor & Francis eBooks

www.taylorfrancis.com

A single destination for eBooks from Taylor & Francis with increased functionality and an improved user experience to meet the needs of our customers.

90,000+ eBooks of award-winning academic content in Humanities, Social Science, Science, Technology, Engineering, and Medical written by a global network of editors and authors.

TAYLOR & FRANCIS EBOOKS OFFERS:

- A streamlined experience for our library customers
- A single point of discovery for all of our eBook content
- Improved search and discovery of content at both book and chapter level

REQUEST A FREE TRIAL
support@taylorfrancis.com